SHOE LEATHER FOR OUR LIFE JOURNEY

To God be the glory!

Ed Thomas

Edwin W. Thomas

CONTENTS

FOREWORD

As a youngster, I accepted Jesus Christ as my savior from sin, primarily to avoid the burning fires of hell. I had no concept of a Sovereign God who loves me more than I love myself. In fact, it was many years after college that I began to realize the undeserved and unconditional love (grace) of God. I began to see that I had been in a one-sided love affair where only my Heavenly Father was bringing love and focused attention to our relationship.

In essence, I was a born-again baby who had never grown spiritually, even though I was physically an adult. God began to grow and mature me in the reality of His love when my wife, Wanda, and I got involved in several Bible studies. God developed a tremendous hunger in me for His Word, and I literally "ate" as much of this spiritual food as I could get from His Word and from hundreds of conservative Biblically-based Christian books, commentaries, and articles.

In a few years, I wanted to share with others what God was teaching me. This was the start of years and years of my teaching and speaking about our loving Heavenly Father who wants each of us to "know" Him (not "know about") so that we can have an eternal, intimate love relationship with Him.

When Wanda went Home to Heaven in early 2022, God brought three different people at different times to encourage me to write **"Life Journey With God"** (basically my autobiography), which was published and released on Amazon in late 2022.

Now God has put it on my heart to write this book, "Shoe Leather For Our Life Journey," to demonstrate the necessity of His Word in our everyday lives in every step we take, every thought that we have, and every choice we make.

The writing in this book comes primarily from volumes of Bible study lessons and materials that I have written, accumulated, and used over years of learning and teaching God's Word. I have added "Some Personal Steps in Shoe Leather" at the end of most chapters to provide my personal involvement in some of the teachings in that chapter. In addition, God has enlightened many other writers/teachers with truth, knowledge, and wisdom from which their books, articles, periodicals, and quotes provided additional valuable insight for this book. God also has provided many different versions of Scripture used in this book. Furthermore, I greatly appreciate the wisdom and many hours of editing and commenting that Peter Forbes, former Founding President of the National Christian Foundation in Houston, provided for this book. **For all of these, I say, "Thank you, and to God be all of the glory."**

INTRODUCTION

Walking barefooted throughout our life brings great pain as we step on rocks and other impediments on the road. A long journey requires having shoe leather to protect our feet. **The strongest and toughest shoe leather is that provided by our loving Heavenly Father—His Word.**

God's shoe leather doesn't remove the obstacles in our journey but provides peace, joy, and comfort as we walk through them. A thin layer of shoe leather is better than bare feet, but a thick layer is necessary for many common obstacles and circumstances which have the potential to cause pain and suffering.

Understanding some **basic shoe leather principles** will help to make our life journey less stressful and arduous. This is shoe leather, without which we would be walking barefooted with all kinds of evil and hurtful things to step on.

(1) The first principle is to come to the realization that **God loves His children and wants what is best for them.** God loves us more than we love ourselves. His love is unconditional and undeserved; it is **GRACE—** God's Riches At Christ's Expense (**Ephesians 2:7**).

God is love (**1 John 4:16**). He owns us (**1 Cor 6:19-20**) and will always do what is "best" for us. Understanding God's "best" for us is difficult because it is so different many times from what we define as "best." Our life journey will be filled with discontentment until we yield to "God's best."

(2) Another primary principle is that **man's view must be aligned with God's view in understanding "time."** God created "time" and is not bound by it. **2 Peter 3:8** tells us that to God, *"one day is like a thousand years and a thousand years are like a day."* **James 4:14** states that our physical life is only a vapor that appears for a little while and then vanishes.

Man is bound by the urgency of time and wants immediate answers from God. Waiting on God is difficult for humans if we look at time in man's view. For example, God promised Abraham, age 75, and Sarah, age 65, a child **(Genesis 15:2-6)**, and 25 years later, God fulfilled that promise **(Genesis 21:1-3)**. God certainly uses His view of time to increase our faith. **Hebrews 11:1** provides us a good definition, *"Faith is the assurance of things hoped for, perceiving as real fact what is not revealed to the senses."*

Eternity will be a timeless, forever existence.

(3) Establish an eternal perspective. It's realizing that even though our time here on earth is temporary, our relationship with Jesus starts now and goes on for eternity. So, no matter what we are facing, Jesus is here with us here and now, and we will be with Him in eternity. He sacrificed His life for us, then He rose again so we too can rise again with Him. **2 Corinthians 4:18** instructs us, *"Do not focus on what is seen, but what is unseen. For what is seen is temporary but what is not seen is eternal."*

God created a perfect world without sin, and in eternity, once again, we will live in that perfect world where the evil of Satan and the sin of man no longer exist. **An eternal perspective is a way of seeing the pain, pleasure, and purpose of our earthly lives as part of the redemptive story God is orchestrating.**

(4) Do not fear physical death. When man originally sinned, man separated Himself from God. God provided the Way back from that separation. **John 14:6** clearly records the statement of Jesus, *"I am the Way, the Truth, and the Life; no man can come to the Father except by Me."*

While we are on this earth, we live in a sinful, fallen world. The primary way into God's perfect eternal world (without sin, evil, pain, suffering, and tears for believers who have accepted Christ as the savior) is through physical death. (The only other way is the rapture described in **1 Thessalonians 4:13-18**.) **For believers, death becomes a friend; for unbelievers, death is an enemy.**

"Without Jesus, we approach life with the expectation of death. With Jesus, we approach death with the expectation of life." — **Nabeel Qureshi**, Pakistani, American Christian apologist

(5) God will not show us what is on the road ahead, but **He will thoroughly equip us for the journey**. His living Presence is our Companion every step of the way. We must stay in constant communication with God and keep our focus on Him. **His abiding Presence is the best road map available (John 16:13-14).**

God in **Isaiah 55:11 encapsulates my heart's desire for this book about the shoe leather of God—His Word,** *"So is my Word that goes out from my mouth: It will not return to me empty, but will accomplish what I desire and achieve the purpose for which I sent it."*

To God be the glory!

CHAPTER 1.

THE SHOE LEATHER OF GOD—HIS WORD

"I want to know one thing, the way to heaven: how to land safe on that happy shore. God Himself has condescended to teach the way; for this very end He came from heaven. He has written it down in a book! Oh, give me that book! At any price, give me the book of God! I have it: here is knowledge enough for me. Let me be: A man of one book." — **John Wesley**, English theologian and evangelist

The Word of God, the Bible, is a masterpiece. It was written over the course of 1,500+ years, roughly between 1450 BC to 95 AD, by as many as 40+ writers under the inspiration of God (*"All scripture is God-breathed."* **2 Timothy 3:16**) and in three main languages—Hebrew, Aramaic, and Koine Greek. It is a collection of 66 books which includes 39 Old Testament books and 27 New Testament books. It documents the rising and falling of major kingdoms throughout history and speaks of the love and sovereignty of our God through it all. But most of all, it is the unshakeable and infallible Word of God. It is God's mouthpiece to us here on earth and is the main resource God has given us to know Him more. It is our vital lifeline that provides shoe leather and power for our life journey.

"In the beginning was the Word, and the Word was with God, and the Word was God." **(John 1:1)**

His Word (1) is eternal, (2) testifies concerning Christ, (3) leads men and women to salvation and regeneration, (4) provides spiritual nourishment to grow, and (5) is practical and applicable (shoe leather for our life journey).

(1)   His Word is eternal.

"The grass withers and the flowers fall, but the Word of God endures forever" **(Isaiah 40:8).**

"Heaven and earth will pass away, but my Word will never pass away" **(Matthew 24:35).**

(2)   His Word testifies concerning Christ.

As we walk through the Bible and down the Golden Road in the next chapter, we will see that God in His first book of the Old Testament, Genesis, provides a clear hint of a Redeemer after man sins and separates himself from God. From the beginning of the Old Testament to the end of the New Testament, the Bible reveals Christ and His redemptive work to save mankind from their sinful separation from God. Jesus in **John 5:39** says, *"You search the Scriptures because you think that in them you have eternal life; and it is these that testify **concerning me**."* After His resurrection, in **Luke 24:44**, Christ told His disciples, *"These are My words which I spoke* *to you while I was still with you, that all the things written in the Law of Moses and the Prophets and Psalms **concerning me** must be fulfilled."* This is a clear statement that means that everything in the Old Testament, which includes the books of the law, the prophets, and the psalms, was written concerning Christ.

"The Word became flesh and made His dwelling among us. We have seen His glory, the glory of the one and only Son, who came from the Father, full of grace and truth" **(John 1:14).**

"The Son is the radiance of God's glory and the exact representation of His being, sustaining all things by His powerful word. After He had provided purification for sins, He sat down at the right hand of the Majesty in heaven" **(Hebrews 1:3).**

(3) His Word leads men and women to salvation and regeneration.

How do we receive salvation? We are saved by faith. *"Faith comes by hearing and hearing by the Word of God"* **(Romans 10:17).** Hearing the good news of redemption through Jesus **(Ephesians 1:7-14).** Then, we must *believe*—fully trust the gospel of Christ and the power of God **(Romans 1:16).** Salvation is available in Jesus alone **(John 14:6; Acts 4:12)** and is dependent on God alone for provision, assurance, and security. *"For by grace* (undeserved and unconditional love*) are you saved through faith; and that is not of yourselves, it is a gift of God. Not of works, lest any man should boast"* **(Ephesians 2:8-9).**

To be regenerated is to be "born again" with God's life. *"Having been regenerated not of corruptible seed but of incorruptible, through the living and abiding Word of God."* **(1 Peter 1:23)** God's Word is the seed of life. When people hear His Word, it plants new life into them. Regeneration is necessary. Sinful human flesh cannot stand in God's presence. In His conversation with Nicodemus, Jesus said twice that a man must be <u>born again</u> in order to see the kingdom of God (**John 3:3, 7**). Regeneration is not optional, for *"flesh gives birth to flesh, but the Spirit gives birth to spirit"* (**John 3:6**).

Physical birth fits us for earth; spiritual rebirth fits us for heaven. Regeneration is part of what God does for us at the moment of salvation, along with sealing which secures our redemption (**Ephesians 1:13-14**), adoption (**Galatians 4:5**), reconciliation (**2 Corinthians 5:18–20**), and redemption (**Romans 3:24, Ephesians 1:7**). Regeneration is God's making a person spiritually alive, because of faith in Jesus Christ. Prior to salvation, we were not God's children (**John 1:12–13**); rather, we were children of wrath (**Ephesians 2:3**). Before salvation, we were degenerate; after salvation, we are regenerated. The result of regeneration is peace with God (**Romans 5:1**), new life (**2 Corinthians 5:17**), and eternal sonship (**John 1:12–13; Galatians 3:26**). Regeneration begins the process of sanctification wherein we become more and more Christlike (**Romans 8:28–30**).

(4)   His Word provides spiritual nourishment to grow.

1 Peter 2:2 says, *"As newborn babies, desire the pure milk of the Word, that you may grow by it."* After babies are born, their immediate need is to be nourished; they need milk to live and grow. The Bible is the milk that can cause us to grow spiritually. After we are regenerated, we are like newborns; our most important need is to come daily to God's Word and drink spiritual milk. Then, just as a baby grows physically from eating well, we'll grow spiritually from His Word. Throughout our Christian lives, we should continue to hunger for and be nourished by the healthy milk of

God's Word. It's a healthy practice to spend time in the Word each day simply to be nourished, but it's essential for new believers to grow in a healthy way.

In **Matthew 4:4,** Jesus said, *"It is written, 'Man shall not live on bread alone, but on every word that proceeds from the mouth of God.'"* The Word of God is not only spiritual milk to us; it is also our spiritual bread of life. We can never sustain ourselves without eating God's Word every day, just as we can never sustain ourselves without eating physical meals each day. Even the Lord Jesus, while He was living as a man on the earth, took God's Word as His bread. So, no matter how much we grow in the divine life as believers, we still need to receive daily nourishment from God's Word to be healthy Christians.

Jeremiah records his experience with God's Word in **Jeremiah 15:16,** *"Your words were found, and I ate them, and Your words became to me the gladness and joy of my heart."* May this be our experience, as well; healthy eating of God's Word that will bring us gladness and joy.

(5) God's Word is practical and applicable (shoe leather for our life journey).

The acronym for **BIBLE** presents some good shoe leather insight—**B**asic **I**nstructions **B**efore **L**eaving **E**arth.

"Everyone who hears these words of mine and puts them into practice is like a wise man who built his house on the rock" (**Matthew 7:24**).

A few verses that highlight the practicality of God's Word include:

"For the word of God is living and powerful, and sharper than any two-edged sword, piercing even to the division of soul and spirit, and of joints and marrow, and is a discerner of the thoughts and intents of the heart" **(Hebrews 4:12).**

"All Scripture is God-breathed and is useful for teaching, rebuking, correcting and training in righteousness, so that the servant of God may be thoroughly equipped for every good work" **(2 Timothy 3:16-17).**

"God's word is a lamp for my feet, a light on my path" **(Psalm 119:105).**

"The unfolding of God's words gives light; it gives understanding to the simple" **(Psalm 119:130).**

"How can a young person stay on the path of purity? By living according to God's Word" **(Psalm 119:9).**

"For the Lord gives wisdom; from his mouth comes knowledge and understanding" **(Proverbs 2:6).**

Applying the Bible is the duty of all Christians. If we don't apply it, the Bible becomes nothing more to us than a normal book, an impractical collection of old manuscripts. In essence, we do not have the shoe leather to travel our life journey; we are barefooted in an evil world of dangers and obstacles. The degree to which we study, memorize, and meditate on God's Word is the degree to which we understand how it applies to our lives which will add shoe leather to our journey. But understanding how the Word applies is not enough; we must actually apply it **(James 1:22)** by making practical use of the shoe leather. "Application" implies action and obedient action is the final step in causing God's Word to come to life in our lives.

As a final word, it is important to note that we are not alone in our trying to understand and apply God's Word to our lives. God has indwelled us with His Spirit (**John 14:16-17**), who speaks to us, leading and guiding us into all truth (**John 16:13**). For this reason, Paul instructs believers to "*walk by the Spirit*" (**Galatians 5:16**), "*for He is a very present Help in our time of need*" (**Psalm 46:1**). The Spirit will faithfully guide us into the will of God, always teaching us to do what is right (**Ezekiel 36:26-28; Philippians 2:13**). Who is better to teach how to live according to all that is written in the Bible than the One who inspired the Bible to begin with—the Holy Spirit Himself? Therefore, let us do our part by hiding the Word in our hearts and obeying the Holy Spirit as He puts God's Word into shoe leather.

Someone once asked **Billy Graham**, "*If Christianity is valid, why is there so much evil in the world?*" To this he replied, "*With so much soap, why are there so many dirty people in the world? Christianity, like soap, must be personally applied if it is to make a difference in our lives.*"

One personal application to make a difference in our Christian lives is to use **S.O.A.P.** to get more out of our time in God's Word. It is an effective way to allow the Holy Spirit to add shoe leather to your life journey. **S.O.A.P.** stands for **S**cripture, **O**bservation, **A**pplication, and **P**rayer.

S – Scripture

Write down in a journal the Bible passage (one verse or several) you'll be studying. If you are just beginning, I would recommend starting with the gospel of John. Writing helps you to focus on each word individually and on the passage as a whole. It allows you to soak it in and meditate on it.

O – Observation

What do you think God is saying to you in this Scripture? Ask the Holy Spirit to teach you and reveal Jesus to you. Paraphrase and write this Scripture down in your own words in your journal.

A – Application

Personalize what you have read by asking yourself how it applies to your life right now. Perhaps it is instruction, encouragement, a revelation of a new promise, or corrections for a particular area of your life. Write how this Scripture can apply to you today.

P – Prayer

This can be as simple as asking God to help you use this Scripture, or it may be a greater insight into what He may be revealing to you. Prayer is a two-way conversation, so be sure to listen to what God has to say. Now, write it out.

"If the Bible is a book of inspirational stories and helpful principles but is devoid of any power to fix what is broken, it is another inspiration devotional book worth little." — **Paul David Tripp,** Pastor, author, and conference speaker

Every person's life journey is difficult with all kinds of problems because we live in a fallen evil world. Our loving Heavenly Father has provided His Word to provide the necessary shoe leather and the power to walk on and through these obstacles. To assume that you do not need the power of His Word is to blindly believe that you have no problems and obstacles in which you need help and support.

SOME PERSONAL STEPS IN SHOE LEATHER

As I stated in the Foreword, I did not start to grow spiritually until God's Word became a crucial part of my daily life. It was through this regular involvement that I personally experienced God's love and His intimacy. I praise God for opening my eyes so that I could finally see.

CHAPTER 2.
WALK THROUGH THE BIBLE (THE BIG PICTURE)

One of the best ways to start our life journey is to understand the Big Picture of the Bible as we walk with God. He unfolds His story of creation, fall, redemption, and love that weaves its way through all 66 books. In this Walk Through the Bible, we see that God redeems (buys back) what was originally given and lost due to man's freedom of choice, either to separate from God or choose to be with God for eternity. What God started in creation with a perfect, sin-free world, He plans to redeem, including all those who choose to accept His only way of redemption through Jesus Christ—the Messiah, Redeemer, and Savior.

Author of the Bible

If you journey with someone, you should know them. To understand The Big Picture of the Bible, we must understand the author, God. Even though forty or so writers wrote the books in the Bible, **2 Timothy 3:16** tells us that God inspired each writing and was the overall author. God is sovereign; He is in total control of His creation. God is perfect within

Himself. He needs nothing to make Himself more perfect. He created all things for His pleasure (**Revelation 4:11**), not out of any need. He is not bound or controlled by any of His creations, including "time,"; so, He sees all things throughout eternity as if they are all current (past, present, and future). He loves you more than you love yourself, and He wants the very best for you. He is invisible to man, but many invisible things with power (electricity, wind, air that we breathe, etc.) are brought to reality by the results they bring.

OLD TESTAMENT

Creation of angels

God creates angels (**Job 38:4-7, Psalms 148:2-5, 104:2-5**). One-third of the angels follow Lucifer in eternal rebellion against their Creator and fall from His grace. Lucifer is renamed Satan (also referred to as the Devil, the Destroyer, the Deceiver) (**Isaiah 14:12-14, Ezekiel 28:13-17, 2 Peter 2:4, Revelation 12:4**). Unholy (fallen) angels are referred to as demons in the Bible.

Creation of the world

Genesis 1 & 2; The most popular theory of secularists for creation is the Big Bang Theory, where a big mass explodes into all the galaxies, planets, and stars. (As much of a chance as my dynamiting a pile of junk into a Rolls Royce.) The Hebrew word for create "bara" in **Genesis** means to make something out of nothing. (Secularists need to answer where in their theory that big mass came from that exploded.) Only God can "bara." The Earth is in the Milky Way Galaxy, which, as reported by Wikipedia, is up to 200,000 light years from rim to rim (one light year=6 trillion miles); our galaxy contains 100–400 billion stars, many larger than our sun, which is 110 times larger than Earth. Currently, an estimated 200 billion observable galaxies like the Milky Way exist.

The magnitude and order of creation continue to amaze scientists. Each created thing breaks down further and further into more parts. The human body is made up of atoms and molecules, which are further broken down into electrons and a nucleus, which contains protons and neutrons. (Secularists promote that evolution was responsible for putting all these submicroscopic elements together in the proper order to make humans with amazing brains; they rationalize that "millions of years of evolving" provide the answer.)

Creation should bring us to our knees at the awesome greatness of God.

Creation of Man

Genesis 1:26-31, 2:15-17 God gives man four major attributes, including (1) dominion over the earth, (2) the image of God, (3) a personal relationship with God, and (4) a body that was intended to live eternally. Man was created "good" and with freedom of choice; he could choose to obey or disobey God. Man would have remained good in God's eyes throughout eternity if he had not chosen to disobey God.

Man Falls

Genesis 3:1-13 Satan, the serpent, entices man to question God's word and His goodness: man, as a result, chooses to disobey God in the one no-no that God provided. Even though eating a fruit seems innocent and does not rank on our radar screen of crime, it was a deliberate choice to disobey God- which was a sin (an archer's term meaning to miss the target).

Man loses dominion, the divine part of the image of God (righteousness and holiness), the personal relationship with God, and death is instituted.

Satan temporarily usurps the dominion of Earth (**Matthew 4:8-9; John 12:31, 14:30, 16:11; 2 Corinthians 4:4**).

God provides a Plan of Redemption

The entire Bible gives us the Plan written by God prior to the foundation of Earth (**Revelation 13:8, Ephesians 1:4, 2 Timothy 1:9**), whereby He provides man "the Way" to redeem what was lost in the Fall. The Old Testament and the New Testament weave the Plan to be fulfilled through a Redeemer (Messiah), who is first hinted at in **Genesis 3:15** immediately after the Fall.

The Old Testament paves a **Messianic Golden Road** on which we will shortly walk at the end of the Old Testament Overview (later in this chapter). God, in His grace, instituted a sacrificial, substitutionary atonement where man may be redeemed based on the shedding of blood (Redemption requires a blood sacrifice). Since Satan and the demons do not have omniscience (all knowledge) and must live bound by creation, this Plan to redeem humans was an unpleasant surprise. Their evil objective was to thwart this Plan to stop the Plan prematurely by eliminating the Redeemer indirectly throughout his genealogy before his birth or directly after his birth. Failing at this, they use their evil and temporary dominion over this earth to try to keep every human from being redeemed and to fight against each redeemed human (**Ephesians 6:12**).

Flood

Unconfessed sin builds on itself. Man's thoughts were evil continually. God sends a universal flood to destroy all but a remnant approximately 1,636 years after creation. God's remnant that He saved was Noah, his wife, his three sons (Ham, Shem & Japheth), and their wives, plus the animals (**Genesis 6, 7 & 8**). After 371 days in the ark, God tells the eight to leave the ark and to be fruitful, multiply and replenish the earth (**Genesis 9**).

Disbursing Nations

Instead of obeying God to spread out to fill the earth, the eight head back to where their home was before the flood. One hundred years after the flood, God forces them to obey by confusing their one language into many. Japheth's descendants headed north (Eastern and Western Europe), Ham's descendants headed east and south (Asia and Africa), and Shem's descendants stayed in the middle east and northern part of Africa (**Genesis 11**).

Abraham

This descendant of Shem was born about 200 years after the disbursing of the nations. God makes an unconditional covenant with Abraham (**Genesis 12:1-3**), promising him three things—**land, seed, and blessing**. Since he was 75 years of age and his wife, Sarah, was 65 years of age with no children, the promise of a seed was unbelievable, made even more so by the fact that he would be in the lineage of the Redeemer. The genealogy of the Redeemer is recorded in two different places in the Bible—the first recording of his earthly father's genealogy is in **Matthew 1:1-16,** and the second recording of his mother's genealogy is in **Luke 3:23-38.** Abraham had two sons—Ishmael and Isaac (in the Redeemer's line); Isaac had two sons—Esau and Jacob (in the Redeemer's line); Jacob (whose name was changed by God to Israel) had twelve sons; through Judah, the Redeemer's line continues.

However, the son of Israel that is written about the most is the next to youngest—Joseph. He was sold into slavery by his brothers because they were jealous of his being Israel's favorite son. He was age seventeen when he was taken to Egypt, and for thirteen years was a slave, most of the time in prison. Through the sovereignty of God, at age thirty, Joseph became the second most powerful man in Egypt. God used Joseph to be the protector of his family. In fact, Joseph describes a perfect spiritual vision in **Genesis 50:20** (perfect human vision is 20:20) to his brothers when he says, *"You meant it for evil, God used it for good in order to save many people"* — a true demonstration of God's sovereignty.

Moses

Joseph dies, and one of the next Pharaohs puts the family of Israel into slavery, which lasts for about 400 years. God raises Moses to deliver the Israelites out of bondage. God aims ten plagues at the Egyptian gods to show His power. Passover is instituted by God to show that the shed blood of an innocent lamb provides deliverance to those believing and death to the unbelievers. However, blood sacrifice was first instituted by God in the Garden of Eden after the Fall when God provided the covering (atonement) for Adam and Eve (**Genesis 3:21**). The shedding of blood is necessary for redemption/deliverance (**Leviticus 17:11, Hebrews 9:22**).

Mosaic Covenant—The Law

After God divides the Red Sea for the Israelites to cross to the Sinai Peninsula, God provides the Law (10 commandments for moral and 603 rules for civil and ceremonial purposes) not as a means of justification/redemption but as a rule for living and preparatory discipline, a schoolmaster to point to the Redeemer (**Galatians 3:19-25**). This covenant was "conditional" on the obedience of the people (**Exodus 19:5**), unlike the Abrahamic Covenant, which was unconditional and based solely on God's promise.

Wilderness

Twelve spies were sent into the Promise Land; ten came back with a negative report that there were giants in the land that would mash Israel like grasshoppers; two, Joshua and Caleb, advised them to believe in God and take the land. As a result of following the advice of the faithless ten and avoiding the land, God judged that Israel would roam in the wilderness for forty years until every male over twenty years of age died—about 600,000 of them.

Joshua

Under the leadership of 85-year-old Joshua, the nation enters the promised land; prior to entering, Moses gives the law a second time (Deuteronomy means second giving of the law), and God also gives the Palestinian Covenant (**Deuteronomy 29 & 30**) to further explain the "land" portion of the Abrahamic Covenant. God miraculously divides the waters of the Jordan River, allowing the nation to crossover; Moses dies at age 120 prior to crossing. God wants to show the nation that it must always have faith in only God; the first battle at Jericho is won by God supernaturally to demonstrate His power that is available through faith. With the faith of Joshua, the nation of Israel, through many battles, repossessed the Promised Land again after 400+ years.

Judges

At age 110, Joshua dies. For the next several decades, the nation was under a theocracy (ruled by God). During this time, God raises up twelve men (Gideon and Samson, best known) and one woman, Deborah, to judge the will of God in each situation. This time in history recorded much chaos as each person did what was right in his own eyes.

Kings

The turmoil became so great that the people asked Samuel for a king to rule over them. Since it was not yet God's timing for a king, God said no. God allowed the people's choice of Saul as their first king because he was handsome, tall, and a good orator. As a result, their human choice is a terrible king. God chooses His king based not on the outward appearance but on the inward heart. David, a teenage shepherd who was even the last of his brothers that his earthly dad considered worthy, was chosen by God to become the second king.

God further explains the "seed" portion of the Abrahamic Covenant to David in the Davidic Covenant (**2 Samuel 7:12-16**); through his seed, Solomon, the right to the throne shall descend (Joseph, Jesus' earthly father, is in this line as written in the genealogy in **Matthew 1**). Through another son of David, Nathan, Mary's genealogy flows (**Luke 3:23-38**).

Solomon's son, Rehoboam, is the next king; he desires to be greater than Solomon, so he increases taxes *"like the finger is to the forearm"*; the people rebel, and the kingdom splits with the northern ten tribes of Israel under the leadership of a general named Jeroboam and the southern two tribes, Judah, and Benjamin, under Rehoboam. The northern kingdom, after 200 years, is taken into captivity by Assyria, and the southern kingdom, after 300 years, is taken into captivity by Babylon.

Prophets

During the time of the split kingdom, God called special men as prophets with primarily a two-fold job—first, to forthtell God's word to warn against worshipping false gods and to obey God; and second, to foretell revealed events by God in the future. God used the prophets to lead His people away from sin and back on the path of righteousness. Many of these prophets predicted and foresaw the coming Messiah, who was prophesied to be the long-awaited Savior and liberator of His people. A large portion of the Old Testament is comprised of the books of these prophets.

SUMMARY OF OLD TESTAMENT PROPHETS

Prophet	Time Period	Setting	Theme
Isaiah	BC 739-681	Pre-exile: Judah	Salvation is of the Lord (Israel's Messiah)
Jeremiah	BC 627-575	Pre-exile: Judah	Warning of Coming Judgment
(Lamentations)	BC 586-575		
Ezekiel	BC 593-571	Exile:Captives in Babylonia	Judgement and Glory of the Lord
Daniel	BC 605-536	Exile: Captives in Babylonia	Sovereignty of God over men and nations
Hosea	BC 760-700	Pre-exile: Israel	Loyal love of God
Joel	BC 841-834	Pre-exile: Judah	Day of the Lord
Amos	BC 760-753	Pre-exile: Israel	Judgment on Sin
Obadiah	BC 850-840	Pre-exile: Edom	Doom of Edom
Jonah	BC 785-750	Pre-exile: Assyria	God's Mercy-Salvation to the Gentiles
Micah	BC 735-700	Pre-exile: Judah	Injustice of Judah and Justice of God
Nahum	BC 660-620	Pre-exile: Assyria	The Destruction of Nineveh
Habakkuk	BC 609-603	Pre-exile: Judah	The Just shall Live by Faith (From Doubt to Faith)
Zephaniah	BC 640-620	Pre-exile: Judah	Judgment and Blessing in the Day of the Lord
Haggai	BC 520	Post-exile: Jews who returned to Jerusalem from Babylonia	Rebuilding the Temple
Zechariah	BC 520-480	Post-exile: Jews who returned to Jerusalem from Babylonia	Messiah's Advents and Future Blessing for Israel
Malachi	BC 433-420	Post-exile: Jews who returned to Jerusalem from Babylonia	Appeal to Backsliders

Return from captivity.

After seventy years in captivity, Cyrus, king of Persia, frees the people from the southern kingdom to return to Jerusalem to rebuild the Temple and the walls of the city under the leadership of Ezra, Nehemiah, and Zerubbabel. Only about 50,000 choose to return.

This is the historical end of the Old Testament.

MESSIANIC GOLDEN ROAD through Old Testament Scriptures.

Before continuing our Walk Through the New Testament, it is also important to take a Scriptural view of the Messianic Golden Road that God has paved through the Old Testament to look at "many" of the 300-plus hints, foreshadows, and predictions of the coming Messiah. The Old Testament was written to create an anticipation of and pave the way for the coming of Christ. It is the story of the Hebrew Nation, dealing largely with events and exigencies of its own times. But all through the Story, there runs unceasing expectancy and vision of the coming of the Messiah, who will rule and bless the whole world.

The Messianic Golden Road is paved through these verses. It extends through and binds together many diverse books into one amazing unity. Starting with vague hints, there soon begin to appear specific, definite predictions, which, as the story sweeps onward, become more specific, more definite, and more abundant. The following Old Testament passages most plainly point forward to the Coming of Christ and pave that Golden Road on which we will take a side trip in our journey.

Genesis 3:15. Seed of the Woman *"Seed of the Woman shall bruise the Serpent's Head. Serpent shall bruise "HIS" heel."* This seems to say that God is determined, despite man's sin, to bring His creation of man to a successful Issue. As through woman, man fell; so, through woman shall man be redeemed. It will be by a Man, "HIS," who will be of the Seed of the Woman, that is, born of a woman without the agency of a man. It is a primeval hint of the Virgin Birth of Christ. For there has been only ONE descendant of Eve, who was born of a woman without being begotten by man.

Genesis 4:3-5. Abel's Offering *"Cain brought of the fruit of the ground an offering to the Lord and Abel brought of the firstlings of his Flock. . . And the Lord had respect unto Abel and his offering. But unto Cain offering he had no respect."* This looks like the institution of Blood Sacrifice, right at the start, as the condition of man's acceptance by God—a primal Hint and the beginning of a long line of pictures and predictions of Christ's Atoning Death for human sin.

Genesis 12:3; 18:18; 22:18. Call of Abraham *"In Thee shall all the nations of the earth be blessed."* Here is a clear, definite statement, stated three times, to Abraham, that in him God was founding a nation for the express purpose to, through this nation, be a blessing to all nations. In time it came to be called the Messianic Nation.

Genesis 14:18-20. Melchizedek, King of Salem, Priest of God, brought bread and wine and blessed Abraham. And Abraham gave tithes to Melchizedek. In **Psalm 110:4,** it is said of the coming Messiah, *"Thou art a Priest forever after the order of Melchizedek."* In **Hebrews 7,** Melchizedek, as a King-Priest, is called a type of Jesus. So, here we have a sort of historical shadow-picture of the coming super-human person whom Abraham's Nation was being formed to bring into the world as the Savior of mankind. And it was in Salem, that is, Jerusalem, the same city where Jesus was crucified.

Genesis 22:1-19. Abraham Offers Isaac A Father offering his son as a substitutionary sacrifice (**22:13**). And it was on Mount Moriah (**22: 2**), the same mount on which Jesus was crucified, and the same place where Abraham had paid tithes to Melchizedek (**14: 18**), Salem being on Mount Moriah. As Melchizedek seems to have been a primeval shadow, in Abraham's life, of the person Abraham's nation would bring into the world, so here seems to be shadow of the event in the coming person's life by which He would do His work. What an apt picture of the death and resurrection of Christ (**Hebrews 11:17-19**).

Genesis 26:4; 28:14. The Promise Repeated Made three times to Abraham, it is here repeated to Isaac, and then to Jacob, that their seed would be a Blessing.

Genesis 49:10-11. Shiloh The Scepter shall not depart from Judah till Shiloh comes. And unto Him shall the gathering of the people be. He washed His garments in the blood of grapes. Here is the first clear, definite prediction that ONE PERSON would arise in Abraham's Nation to rule all nations, Shiloh, He whose right It Is. He must be the one of whom Melchizedek was a shadow. He would appear in the tribe of Judah. His garments washed in the blood of grapes, may be a metaphorical indication of His crucifixion.

Exodus 12. Institution of the Passover

Israel's deliverance out of Egypt. Death of Egypt's firstborn. Israel's houses marked with the blood of a lamb. The Lord passed over those so marked. The feast to be kept annually throughout all their generations. It became Israel's principal feast to observe in memory of the deliverance from Egypt.

Kept for 1,400 years as the very heart of the Hebrew Nation. Unmistakably, it was designed by God to be a gigantic historical fore-picture of the basic event of human Redemption, the death of Christ, the LAMB OF GOD, who expired on the Cross at a Passover Feast, bringing Eternal Deliverance from sin, for those marked with His blood, even as the first Passover brought deliverance from Egypt for Israel. It shows how much God's plan was for the coming of Christ long before He came.

Leviticus 16. The Day of Atonement

Once each year on the tenth day of the seventh month in the Hebrew calendar (usually September or October), two goats were taken; one was killed as a sin offering, and the High Priest laid hands on the second, a scapegoat, confessing over him the people's sins. The scapegoat was led away and let go into the wilderness. This and the whole Levitical sacrifices, as continuing features of Hebrew life, are clear historical indications of the atoning death of the coming Messiah.

Numbers 21:6-9. The Fiery Serpent

In the wilderness, serpents bit the people; many died. Moses made a serpent of brass which was a symbol of sin judged, and bronze is divine judgment. Whoever looked at it lived. Jesus took this picture of Himself being lifted upon the cross (**John 3:14-15**). Mankind bitten with sin in the Garden of Eden may look to Him and live.

Numbers 24:17,19. The Star

There shall come a Star out of Jacob. A Scepter shall rise out of Israel. He shall have dominion. Here is another definite prediction of a person, a brilliant ruler: evidently meaning the same person as the Shiloh of **Genesis 49: 10**, who is to rule the Nations.

Deuteronomy 18:15-19. A Prophet Like unto Moses

God would raise up a Prophet like unto Moses, through whom God would speak to mankind. Evidently, this is another characterization of the Shiloh and the Star aforementioned. Thus, in the first five books of the Old Testament, there is a specific prediction, repeated five times, that the Hebrew nation was being launched into the world for the one express purpose of Blessing All Nations. And also specific predictions that there would arise in the Nation one person, called Shiloh, a Star, a Prophet, with rather plain intimations that it would be through this one person that the Nation would fulfill its mission. Also, there are various hints about the nature of this person's work, especially featuring His sacrificial death. Thus early, 1,400 years before Christ came, there were drawn, in distinct lines, some leading characteristics of Christ's Life.

Joshua (Name means "Jehovah is salvation"). This book seems to have no direct prediction of the Messiah, though Joshua himself is thought, in a sense, to have been typical of Jesus. The names are the same, "Jesus" being the Greek form of the Hebrew "Joshua." As Joshua led Israel into the Promised Land, so Jesus will lead His people into the Promised Heaven.

Ruth. She was the great-grandmother of David, the family from which the Messiah would come. (**Matthew 1:5**) Boaz was of Bethlehem. Jesus was born in Bethlehem. An old tradition has it that Boaz took Ruth to be his bride and started the family, which was to bring Christ into the world in the very same place in which, 1,100 years later, Christ was born.

I Samuel 16. David

He was anointed King over Israel. From here on, David is the central figure of Old Testament History. The most specific and most abundant of all Messianic prophecies cluster around his Name. As Abraham was the founder of the Messianic Nation, David is the founder of the Messianic family within the Nation.

2 Samuel 7:16. David Promised an Eternal Throne

"Thy Throne shall be established forever." Here begins a long line of promises that David's family should reign forever over God's people. This Promise is repeated over and over, throughout the rest of the Old Testament, with an ever-increasing mass of detail, and specific explanations, that the promise will find its ultimate fulfillment in ONE GREAT KING, who will Himself personally live forever and establish a Kingdom of Endless

Duration. This Eternal King, evidently, is the same person previously spoken of as Priest after the order of Melchizedek, Shiloh, Star, and Prophet like unto Moses.

1 Kings 9:5. The Promise Repeated to Solomon

"I will establish the Throne of Thy Kingdom forever." Repeated over and over to David and Solomon. However, the books of **Kings** and **Chronicles** relate the story of the fall of David's Kingdom and the captivity of the Hebrew Nation, apparently bringing into question God's promise to David's family of an Eternal Throne. But in the period covered by these books, many prophets arose, crying out that the Promise would yet be fulfilled. The books of **Ezra, Nehemiah**, and **Esther** relate the story of the return of the fallen and scattered Hebrew Nation without direct Messianic predictions. However, the re-establishment of the Nation in its own land was a necessary antecedent to the fulfillment of promises about David's Throne.

Job 19:25-27. The book of **Job** is a discussion of the problem of suffering, without much direct bearing, as far as we can see, on the Messianic mission of the Hebrew nation, except it is in Job's exultant outburst of faith, *"I know that my Redeemer lives, and that He shall stand at the latter day upon the Earth."*

Psalms. The book of Psalms, written mostly by David himself, is full of predictions and foreshadows of the Eternal King to arise in David's family. Some of them, in a limited and secondary sense, may refer to David himself. But, in the main, they are inapplicable to any person in history other than Christ: written 1,000 years before Christ came.

Psalm 2. The Lord's Anointed Evidently references the Eternal King to arise in David's family. A very positive statement relating to His Deity, His universal reign, and the blessedness of those who trust Him.

Psalm 16:10. His Resurrection *"Thou wilt not suffer thy Holy One to see corruption."* This is quoted in **Acts 2:27, 31** as referring to the Resurrection of Christ. There had been many hints of the coming Messiah's death. Here is a clear-cut prediction of His victory over death and life forevermore.

Psalm 22. Picture of Christ's Future Crucifixion *"My God, My God, why have you forsaken me?"* Even His dying words foretold (**Matthew 27:46**), *"All that see Me laugh at Me to scorn, saying…He trusted in God, let God deliver Him."* Sneers of His enemies in their exact words (**Matthew 27:43**), *"They pierced My hands and feet."* This indicates crucifixion as the manner of His death. (**John 20:20, 25**) *"They part my garments among them, and they cast lots upon My vesture"* Even this detail is forecast (**Matthew 27:35**). This Psalm written a thousand years before it happened can only refer to Christ's crucifixion.

Psalm 41:9. To be Betrayed by a Friend *"My own familiar friend, in whom I trusted, who did eat my bread, lifted up his heel against me."* Apparently, David is referring to his own friend, Ahithophel (**2 Samuel 15:12**), but Jesus quoted it as a picture and prophecy of His own betrayal by Judas (**John 13:18-27; Luke 22:47- 48**).

Psalm 45. Reign of God's Anointed (4) *"In Majesty ride on prosperously"* **(6)** *"Thy throne, O God, is forever and ever"* **(7)** *"Thy God hath anointed Thee with oil of gladness above thy fellows."* **(17)** *"All generations…shall praise Thee forever and ever."* Here is depicted the glorious reign of a King, bearing the

Name of God, seated on an Eternal Throne. It can refer to no other than the Eternal King to arise in David's family. A nuptial song of Christ and His Bride, the Church.

Psalm 69:21. Gall and Vinegar *"They gave me gall for my food; and in my thirst they gave me vinegar to drink."* Another incident in the future of the Coming Messiah's sufferings (**Matthew 27:34, 48; John 19:28-30**).

Psalm 72. His Glorious Reign (7) *"In His days the righteous shall flourish."* (8) *"He shall have dominion from sea to sea, and from the river to the ends of the Earth."* (11) *"All kings shall fall down before Him: all nations shall serve Him."* (19) *"Blessed be His glorious Name forever. Let the whole Earth be filled with His Glory."* This Psalm seems, in part, to have been a description of the reign of Solomon. But some of its statements, and its general tenor, surely refer to ONE greater than Solomon.

Psalm 78:2. To Speak in Parables *"I will open My mouth in parables."* Another detail of the Messiah's life, His method of teaching in parables. (Quoted in **Matthew 13:34- 35** as fulfilling this verse.)

Psalm 89. Endlessness of David's *Throne* (3) *"I have made a covenant with David."* (4) *"I will build up Thy throne unto all generations."* (27) *"I will make Him, My First Born, higher than the kings of the Earth."* (28) *"And My covenant shall stand."* (35-36) *"By My Holiness I have sworn …David's Throne... shall endure forever."* God's Oath repeated over and over, for the endlessness of David's Throne, under God's Firstborn.

Psalm 110. Messiah to be King and Priest (1) *"The Lord said to my Lord, sit Thou at My right hand, till I make thine enemies thy footstool"* (**Matthew**

22:42-44) (4) *"Thou art a Priest forever after the order of Melchizedek."* **(Hebrews 5:5-6)** Eternal Dominion and Eternal Priesthood of the coming King. Jesus quoted this as referring to Himself.

Psalm 118:22. Messiah to be Rejected by Rulers *"The Stone the builders rejected is become Head of the Corner."* Jesus quoted this as referring to Himself (**Matthew 21:42-44**).

Isaiah 2:2-4. Magnificent Future Vision of Messianic Age *"In the last days, the mountain of the Lord's House shall be established in the top of the mountains . . . And all nations shall flow unto it. And many peoples shall say, Come, let us go up to …the House of the God of Jacob. He will teach us His Ways, and we will walk in His paths. "The Word of the Lord shall go forth from Jerusalem…and the nations… shall beat their swords into plowshares, and their spears into pruninghooks. Nation shall not lift up sword against nation, neither shall they learn war anymore."* Isaiah, pre-eminently, the Old Testament book of Messianic prophecy, in language unsurpassed in all literature, goes into ecstasy over the glories of the reign of the coming Messiah. **Micah 4:1-5** has the same verbiage with one added verse. The Holy Spirit gave both prophets the same revelation because of its surpassing importance.

Isaiah 4:2-6. The Branch of the Lord *"In that day shall the Branch of the Lord be beautiful and glorious."* The Messiah is here represented as a Branch growing up out of the stump of the family Tree of David, becoming a guide and refuge for His people. (Explained more fully in **Isaiah 11:1-10.**)

Isaiah 7:13-14. Immanuel *"O house of David…a virgin shall conceive and shall bear a Son. and shall call His Name Immanuel."* This seems to say that some One, to be called Immanuel, will be born in David's family, of a virgin: evidently meaning the same person as the Branch of **4:2** and **I l:1**, and the Wonderful Child of **9:6**. The Deity of the Child is implied in the name Immanuel, which means "God with Us." Thus, the Virgin Birth and Deity of the Messiah are foretold here. It is quoted in **Matthew 1:23** as referring to Jesus.

Isaiah 9: 1-2,6-7. The Wonderful Child (1-2) *"In Galilee…the people have seen a Great Light."* **(6-7)** *"For unto us a Child is born, unto us a Son is given, and the government shall be upon His shoulder: and His Name shall be called Wonderful, Counselor, Mighty God, Everlasting Father, Prince of Peace. Of the increase of His government and peace there shall be no end, upon the Throne of David, and upon His Kingdom, from henceforth even forever."* This Child, unmistakably, is the ETERNAL KING promised to David's family (**2 Samuel 7:16**): the same Person spoken of centuries earlier as Shiloh, the Star, and the Prophet like unto Moses. His Deity is emphasized here. His ministry to be in Galilee. A very accurate forecast of Jesus.

Isaiah Il:1-10 Reign of the Branch *"There shall come forth a Rod out of the Stem of Jesse, a Branch shall grow out of his roots.* (That is, a Shoot out of the Stump of David's Family tree, meaning the Messiah.) *And the Spirit of the Lord shall rest upon Him, the Spirit of wisdom and understanding. He shall stand for an Ensign to the peoples, and to Him shall the nations gather. He shall smite the earth with the rod of His mouth. And the wolf shall dwell with the lamb. The leopard shall lie down with the kid: and the calf and the young lion and the fatling together. And a little child shall lead them. The cow and the bear shall feed; their young ones shall lie down together; and the lion shall eat straw like the ox . . . They shall not hurt nor destroy in all my holy mountain; for the earth shall be full of the knowledge of the Lord as the waters cover the sea".*

A magnificent description of universal peace in the world under the reign of the Coming Messiah.

Isaiah 25:6-9; 26:1,19. Resurrection of the Dead (6-8) *"In this mountain the Lord . . . will swallow up death in victory and wipe away tears from off all faces."* **(19).** *"In that day…thy dead shall live, my dead body shall rise . . and the Earth shall cast forth the dead."* A forecast of the Resurrection of Jesus in Mt. Zion and of a general Resurrection.

Isaiah 32:1-2. Again, the Reign of the Coming King *"A King shall reign in righteousness . . . A Man (The Man) shall be as a hiding place from the wind, a covert from the tempest, as streams of water in a dry place, and as the shade of a great rock in a weary land."* In **Isaiah 9:6,** the Deity of the Coming King was predicted. Here it is His humanity, a Man, a Man who is a personal refuge to each one of His people from every trouble.

Isaiah 35:5,6. Messiah's Miracles *"Eyes of the blind shall be opened; ears of the deaf shall be unstopped; the lame shall leap…the tongue of the dumb shall sing."* An exact description of Jesus' ministry of miracles.

Isaiah 35:8-10. Messiah's Highway *"A Highway shall be there. . . called the Way of Holiness. The ransomed of the Lord shall return and come to Zion with singing and everlasting joy upon their heads: they shall obtain joy and gladness: sorrow and sighing shall flee away."* Holiness, happiness, singing, joy, no more sorrow, tears forever gone, for the Coming Messiah's people.

Isaiah 40:5,10,11. Messiah's Tenderness (5) *"The Glory of the Lord shall be revealed, and all flesh shall see it together."* **(10)** *"The Lord God will come with a strong hand, and His arm shall rule for Him."* **(11)** *"He shall feed His flock* *like a shepherd: He shall gather the lambs with His arms, and carry them in His bosom, and shall gently lead those that are with young."* Another preview of the glory of Jesus, His power and His gentleness toward the weak of His flock.

Isaiah 42:1-11. Gentiles *"Behold, My Servant... I give Him for a Light to Gentiles. . . The Isles shall wait for His Law. . . And from the end of the Earth they sing unto the Lord a new song."* Israel's Coming King will rule over Gentiles also and cover the whole Earth with songs of praise and joy.

Isaiah 53. The Messiah's Sufferings *"He is despised and rejected of men; a Man of Sorrows and acquainted with grief...He hath borne our griefs and carried our sorrows...He was wounded for our transgressions and bruised for our iniquities . . . With His stripes, we are healed. The Lord hath laid on Him the iniquity of us all... He was oppressed, He was afflicted, yet He opened not his mouth. He is brought as a lamb to the slaughter...He poured out His soul unto death...and bore the sin of many . . .It pleased the Lord to bruise Him to make His soul an offering for sin... And the pleasure of the Lord shall prosper in His Hand... By knowledge of Him shall many be justified."*

The most conspicuous feature in the prophecies about the coming King is that He would be a sufferer. It was hinted at in Abel's sacrifice and in Abraham's offering of Isaac, and vividly portrayed the future institution of the Passover Feast and in the annual Day of Atonement, and some of its details described in **Psalm 22**. And here, in **Isaiah 53**, detail upon detail is added, making the picture more complete. And in chapters **54, 55, 60, and 61** the suffering King fills the Earth with songs of joy. Marvelous forecasts of the Christian era.

Isaiah 60. To be the Light of the World (1) *"Arise, shine; for thy Light is come, and the Glory of the Lord is risen upon thee."* **(2)** *"Darkness shall cover the Earth. ."* **(20)** *"The Lord shall be thine everlasting Light, and the days of thy mourning shall be ended."* In the New Testament, Jesus is repeatedly called the Light of the World **(John 8:12, 9:5, 12:46).**

Jeremiah 23:5-6. The Branch *"The days come, saith the Lord, that I will raise up unto David a righteous Branch...a King... this is His name whereby He shall be called, THE LORD OUR RIGHTEOUSNESS."* As **Isaiah, chapters 4 and 11,** speaks of the coming King as a Branch out of the family of David, so, here, Jeremiah repeats the Name and asserts His Deity.

Ezekiel 34:22-24; 37:24-25. The Prince of the House of David *"My servant David... shall and be...Shepherd of my Flock King over them...and be their Prince forever."* In describing the reign of the Prince, there is given a beautiful picture of the blessed influences arising out of Jerusalem, under the imagery of the life-giving stream issuing from the Temple and flowing out to the whole world, as recorded in **Ezekiel 47: 1-12.**

Daniel 2:44. Christ's Kingdom *"In the days of these kings shall the God of Heaven set up a kingdom, which shall never be destroyed; and the kingdom shall not be left to other people, but it shall break in pieces and consume all these kingdoms, and it shall stand forever."*

Daniel 9:24. Backbone of Bible Prophecy *"Seventy weeks (weeks of years; 490 years) have been decreed for your people and your holy city, to finish the transgression, to make an end of sin, to make atonement for iniquity, to bring in everlasting righteousness, to seal up vision and prophecy and to anoint the most holy place."* Daniel's 70 'weeks' is considered to be the backbone of Bible prophecy and was given to this greatly beloved man of prayer following twenty-one days of godly intercession and deep repentance on behalf of his people, Israel, and their holy city - Jerusalem. And God, in His grace, laid out a 490-year historical roadmap tracing the future destiny of His chosen people, Israel, and their final restoration as 'My people - My inheritance.'

Bible prophecy is a signpost that points us to Jesus. Daniel's vision has its fulfillment in Christ and Him alone. The prophetic Scriptures tell us of His first coming and His future return. Christ is the living Word made flesh, and Christ is the surer Word of prophecy. Through Him, God promised, *"to finish the transgression, to make an end of sin, to make atonement for iniquity, to bring in everlasting righteousness, to seal up vision and prophecy and to anoint the most holy place."* It was through the Cross that Christ finished the transgression of His people, Israel, and made an end to sin, not only for the remnant of His people who will one day look upon Him Whom they pierced but for all who receive the Lord Jesus Christ as their substitute for the penalty of sin and trust in Him as their resurrected Savior.

Hosea 11:1. Calling Out of Egypt *"I called My Son out of Egypt."* This passage illustrates the principle that prophetic utterances often have a latent and deeper meaning than first appears. Israel, nationally, was a son (**Exodus 4:22**), but Christ was the greater Son (**Matthew 2:15**).

Joel 2:28, 32; 3:13-14. The Gospel Era *"I will pour out My Spirit upon all flesh... Whosoever shall call on the Name of the Lord shall be delivered... Put in the sickle. The harvest is Ripe . . . multitudes, multitudes in the Valley of*

Decision." The Messiah will institute an era of world evangelization, under the leadership of the Holy Spirit (**Acts 2:16—21**).

Amos 9:11,12,14. David's Fallen Throne to Rise "*I will bring back the captivity of My people... and I will plant them in their own land...And in that day I will raise up the Tabernacle of David that is fallen...to possess all the nations that are called by My Name*" (**Acts 15:16-17**).

Jonah 1:17. A Sign to Nineveh "*Jonah was in the fish three days and nights.*" Jesus took it to be a three-day picture miracle of His own resurrection from the Tomb, as a sign to the world (**Matthew 12:40**)

Micah 5:2-5. Bethlehem to be Messiah's Birthplace "*Thou, Bethlehem... out of thee shall He come forth that is to be Ruler in Israel; whose goings forth have been ... from everlasting ... He shall be great unto the ends of the Earth. And this Man shall be our peace*" (**Matthew 2:1-6**).

Zechariah (**3:8**) "*I will bring forth My Servant, the BRANCH.*" (**9:9**) "*O Jerusalem, thy King cometh to thee...Lowly, riding upon a colt*" (**Matthew 21:1-5**) (**12:8**) "*In that day the House of David shall be as God.*" (**3:9**) "*I will remove the iniquity in one day* " (**11:12-13**) "*They weighed for my price thirty of the pieces of silver ...and cast them to the potter.*" (**Matthew 26:15; 27:4-10**) (**12:10**) "*They looked upon me whom they have pierced* (**John 19:37**).

Malachi 3:1; 4:5. A Forecast of John the Baptist "*Behold, I will send My messenger. . . Elijah the Prophet before the great day of the Lord... and He shall prepare the way before Me.*" Jesus, in speaking of John the Baptist, in

Matthew 11:7-14 quotes this passage from Malachi and expressly states that it referred to John the Baptist.

As we have walked down the Messianic Golden Road of Old Testament prophecy, we have found Jesus Christ at its center and its circumference, for He is the Alpha and Omega of prophecy, the beginning and the end, the first and the last, forever and ever. It has been calculated that the odds of any one man fulfilling only 8 of these prophecies would be 1 in 100,000,000,000,000,000 (one hundred quadrillions); Jesus fulfilled over 300 prophesies in His earthly ministry.

We will now continue our journey through the Bible.

400 silent years between the Old Testament and the New Testament

The rule of the Persians continued for about 100 more years. The Greeks, under the leadership of Alexander the Great, conquered Persia; his empire was divided up after his death. Antiochus Epiphanes, in his attempt to Hellenize the Jews, sacrificed a pig on the Temple altar and destroyed all the Old Testament books that he could find; the people revolted and started the Maccabean War. The Roman conquest of the world included this area. The New Testament opens under Roman rule. The Apocrypha, containing fifteen books and included in most Catholic Bibles, contains the history of these silent years. However, there is no record of them in canonized scripture.

"We go from Malachi to Matthew in one page of our scriptures, but that one piece of paper that separates the Old Testament from the New Testament represents 400 years of history - 400 years where there wasn't a prophet, 400

years where God's voice wasn't heard. And that silence was broken with the cry of a baby on Christmas night." — **Louie Giglio,** pastor/leader of Passion City Church, Atlanta

THE NEW TESTAMENT

Jesus' First Coming

The redemptive seed hinted at in **Genesis 3** and weaving His *"seed through the woman"* genealogy through the Old Testament and recorded in Mary's genealogy in **Luke 3** becomes clear in the virgin birth of Jesus (the Lord is salvation) Christ (anointed, Messiah), Immanuel (God with us). Jesus' right to the throne comes through the genealogy of his earthly dad, Joseph, recorded in **Matthew 1**.

Through 4000 years of history, both of these genealogies point to one man - Jesus, the Son of Man. Little is known about the first thirty years of Jesus' life except at birth and at age twelve. He begins his public ministry at age thirty, and it lasts for only three years, during which time he trains and teaches twelve disciples. *"He came to fulfill the Law and the prophets not to destroy them"* (**Matthew 5:17**). *"He became a stumbling stone to those who sought to obtain righteousness through works and not through faith"* (**Romans 9:32**).

He becomes a mediator of a better covenant, the one promised to Abraham in the "blessing" portion of that covenant and further revealed in **Jeremiah 31:31-34** as the New Covenant based on the unconditional promises of God (**Hebrews 8:6-13**).

Jesus' Death & Resurrection

Jesus is crucified, is buried for three days, and is resurrected to have victory over death. As a result, believers now will in heaven have a glorified body like the resurrected body of Jesus Christ that will live forever (**Philippians 3:21, 1 Corinthians 15: 35-50**); what was lost in the Fall is redeemed. On the cross Jesus becomes the sacrificial Lamb of God to shed His blood in a once-for-all-eternity blood sacrifice (**Hebrews 9 & 10**).

By faith we are justified (counted righteous by God). We lost righteousness and our personal relationship with God through Adam. And now through Jesus, our Redeemer, we obtain the gift of righteousness and the abundance of grace (unconditional and undeserved love) whereby we can once again have an intimate relationship with God (**Romans 5:17, 21**). "*We can now put on the new man which after God is created in righteousness and true holiness*" (**Ephesians 4:24**).

We lost our divine image of God (righteousness and holiness) and now He recreates and sanctifies us through Christ to conform us back progressively to that image (**Romans 8:28-29, 2 Corinthians 3:18**). Therefore, salvation through Christ (redemption for what was lost) is a process involving justification (salvation from the penalty of sin), sanctification (salvation from the power of sin), and glorification (salvation from the presence of sin).

Holy Spirit

After His resurrection Jesus lived another forty days on this earth (**Acts 1:3**) and was seen by over 500 people during that period (**1 Corinthians 15:6**).

Immediately before His ascension to the right hand of God, He gave His disciples and all believers the Great Commission to be witnesses to evangelize and disciple the world (**Acts 1:8, Matthew 28:18-20**). However, He knew without the power of God, this would be impossible (**Luke 18:27**). So, He promised that the Holy Spirit of God would come upon them to provide them the power of God; a few days later at Pentecost the Holy Spirit came to indwell them.

The Holy Spirit indwells all believers in Jesus Christ (**Romans 8:9, 1 Corinthians 3:16, 6:19-20**) to provide them power to be witnesses of their faith and to live an abundant Christlike life to give glory to God in all things. The filling (yielding to His control) of the Holy Spirit is the central doctrine of progressive sanctification (being conformed to the image of Jesus Christ) (**Ephesians 5:18**). This period of history with the Holy Spirit is the one in which we are currently living.

FUTURE TIMES PROPHESIED IN THE BIBLE

(Chronological order)

Rapture (1 Thessalonians 4:13-17)

Jesus brings all believers both dead and alive home to Heaven.

Judgment (Bema) Seat of Christ (2 Corinthians 5:10, 1 Corinthians 3:11-15, Romans 14:10)

The Bema in the Ancient Greek Olympics was that raised platform where the judge presented awards to the winners of each contest. All believers must appear before the Bema seat of Christ to receive rewards, if any, earned (after accepting Christ as Savior) for good works that bring glory to God (**Matthew 5:16, John 15:8, 1 Corinthians 6:20, 10:31, 1 Peter 4:11**) during their lives as Christians. Believers do not have to appear at the Great White Throne of Judgment to receive condemnation for sin (**Revelation 20:11-15**) because Christ paid for their sin on the cross.

Salvation is a free gift (**Romans 6:23, Ephesians 2:8-9**); rewards are earned by works. In essence, believers have from God an irrevocable contract which has incentive (reward) clauses for good works.

Ezekiel 38- 39 Invasion of Israel by Northern powers, and Arabs

God sovereignly protects Israel and destroys most of the attacking forces. Since a Moslem Mosque, the Dome of the Rock, is currently on the site of the Jewish temple which will be rebuilt; this defeat of the Arabs provides the Jews the site once again. In addition, a world political leader (later to be revealed as the Antichrist) makes a peace agreement for seven years with Israel (**Daniel 9:27**) which begins the period known as the Tribulation.

Tribulation (Daniel 9:25-27)

1. Jews rebuild the temple (**Daniel 9:27; Revelation 11: 1,2; Matthew 24:15**)

2. 144,000 Jewish believers witness to the world (**Revelation 7**) This will complete God's commandment (**Genesis 12:3**) to Abraham to

be a "blessing" to the nations which the Jews for the 4,000 years since the Abrahamic Covenant have failed to do.

3. Two special Old Testament prophets prophesy and have the power to do miracles for the first 3 ½ years of the tribulation. At the end of this time the Antichrist kills them; their bodies lie in the streets of Jerusalem for three days at which time God resurrects them and brings them into heaven as the world watches in terror. No indication is given as to who these two will be. However, only two Old Testament prophets were taken into heaven without experiencing death: perhaps for this reason - Enoch (**Genesis 5:22-24**) and Elijah (**2 Kings 2:11**).

4. Judgments of God - Seven Seals, seven Trumpets and seven Bowls of wrath (**Revelation 6-19**). It appears that God progressively puts the pressure on to force people to either accept Christ or reject Him.

5. Antichrist breaks the seven years covenant with Israel at mid-tribulation, the end of three and one-half years (**Revelation 11:2; 12**).

6. Michael and holy angels expel Satan and his demons from access to heaven at mid-tribulation (**Revelation 12:7-12**).

7. Israel flees into the wilderness (**Revelation 12:6, 14**).

8. Antichrist and False Prophet in power with Satan (False trinity formed) One world government, one world economy and one world religion are formed (**Revelation 13**).

9. Armageddon (**Revelation 16:12-16; 19:11-21**). At the end of the seven years the Antichrist brings armies from all over the world including two hundred million men from the Far East to destroy the Jews and believers in one ultimate battle.

Second Coming of Jesus Christ as King of Kings & Lord of Lords (Revelation 19:11-16)

1.   Defeats the armies of the Antichrist **(Revelation 19:17-19).**

2.   Antichrist and the False Prophet cast into the lake of fire **(Revelation 19:20)**.

3.   Satan bound for 1,000 years **(Revelation 20:1-3)**.

4.   Judgment of individual Gentiles living on the earth at that time **(Matthew 25:31-46)**

5.   Judgment of Israel **(Ezekiel 20:33-44)**.

Millennium (Revelation 20; Ezekiel 40-48; Isaiah 65: 18-25)

Jesus Christ will reign with his saints on this earth for 1,000 years in His Kingdom. (Dominion lost in the Fall reclaimed from the temporary rule of Satan and the "land" portion of the Abrahamic Covenant fulfilled.) It is then (at the start of His 1,000-year reign on earth), that the Lord will rule with a rod of iron.

The kingdom of this world will become the kingdom of our God. The earth will be filled with the knowledge of the glory of the LORD as the waters cover the sea, and the glory of the Lord will fill His Millennial Temple - so beautifully described by Ezekiel. This will be a time where Jesus Christ as King of Kings controls the media, all governments, the education system and curriculum, the entertainment industry, etc. He rules harshly against open sin and rebellion.

In the beginning of the Millennium only believers will be allowed to be citizens of the Kingdom; however, the population will multiply during this time. Each of these newborn children still must individually choose to accept Jesus Christ as their Savior.

Satan loosed for a short time after the 1,000 years (Revelation 20:7-9).

Perhaps the saddest commentary on the depravity of man in the entire Bible is this passage. Even though the newborn children grow up in a "perfect" utopia with no crime, no bad outside influences, teaching of only absolute truth, etc. under the rule of the King of Kings, many of them (the number of whom is as the sand of the sea) reject Jesus Christ.

They are deceived by Satan to follow him in a final battle in one last attempt to defeat the Eternal Plan of Redemption of God through Jesus Christ. God destroys the unbelievers with fire from heaven and casts Satan into the lake of fire to join the Antichrist and the False Prophet.

Final Judgment for those to be cast into the lake of fire for eternity.

1. Fallen angels (demons) - Saints/believers will participate in this judgment of angels (**1 Corinthians 6:3, Jude 6-7**).

2. Great White Throne judgment of all unbelievers throughout the history of the earth. (**Revelation 20:11-15**).

Earth and heavens burned and purged with fire (2 Peter 3:10-12)

Eternal Kingdom for Believers in Jesus Christ-Everything made new.

1. New heaven and new earth (**2 Peter 3:13, Revelation 21:1**)

2. New Jerusalem (**Revelation 21**)

Believers' home for eternity will be on the new earth. It will be cube shaped with 1,380 miles in each direction. And our glorified bodies apparently will allow traveling vertically, as well as horizontally. One mathematician calculated if 20 billion people accept Christ as Savior, then this new city will allow each person to have seventy-five acres in each cubical direction as his/her individual eternal home. This assumes that 25% is used for inhabitants and 75% is used for common areas.

1. Triune God to dwell among His eternal family and reign on the throne eternally in New Jerusalem (**Revelation 21:3, 22:1-5**).

2. Curse removed—no more tears, no more death, no more sorrow, no more crying, no more pain. Everything made new will remain new throughout eternity (**Revelation 21:4**).

3. New paradise with a river of water of life and the tree of life on both sides of the river (**Revelation 22:1-5**).

4. No more darkness and night, no more light from the sun, God will give the only light needed for eternity (**Revelation 22:5**).

The summary of the Bible is that the one true God displays His glory in redeeming and restoring His fallen creation by fulfilling covenant promises and commands through the glorious person and atoning work of Jesus Christ.

SOME PERSONAL STEPS IN SHOE LEATHER

I have been privileged in almost every extended Bible study that I have taught in the last few decades, to begin with, this "Walk Through the Bible." It is always exciting to see eyes being opened to God's truth and a growing enthusiasm for His Word by almost every participant.

Every time I take this "Walk" and journey down the "Messianic Golden Road," it fills me with awe and wonders at this redemption story of God's love for humanity and the sacrifice He was willing to make for all of mankind to save His people (including me) for His glory. Thank You, God!!!!

CHAPTER 3.
JESUS, DEATH, AND RESURRECTION—FACT OR FICTION

As a Christian author, **Scott Whitaker** wrote about Jesus. *"Jesus worked in a carpenter shop until He was thirty. Then for three years, He was an itinerant preacher. He never went to college or to seminary. Never wrote a book or owned a home. He never lived in a big city or traveled any farther than two hundred miles from His birthplace in Bethlehem. He did none of the things that usually accompany greatness.*

He was thirty-three when the tide of public opinion turned against him. His friends ran away and denied him. He went through the mockery of a trial and was nailed to a cross between two thieves. Dying, his executioners gambled for his garments, his only property on earth, and then He was laid in a borrowed tomb.

He had no trophies to put on a table, no resumes or awards to frame and put on the wall. All the important people of any society, throughout any time in history, probably wouldn't have taken His call. He had no credentials.

Twenty centuries have come and gone, and today He is the One who is the central figure of the human race. And we are well-aligned with truth to say that all the armies that ever marched, all the navies that ever sailed, all the parliaments that ever sat, all the kings that ever reigned—put together—have not affected the life of humanity on this earth as much as that One solitary life - Jesus Christ."

Virtually all scholars of antiquity, both Christian and non-Christian, accept that Jesus of Nazareth was a historical figure, and attempts to deny his historicity have been consistently rejected by the scholarly consensus as a fringe theory. There is just too much evidence to the contrary.

Every major religious movement considers Jesus to be an important religious figure, including Christianity, Islam, Judaism, Baha'i Faith, and Druze Faith. In addition, some high-level Buddhists have drawn analogies between Jesus and Buddhism.

Muslims acknowledge the impact of Jesus and recognize Him as a significant person within their own religious system. The Quran describes Jesus in the following ways: born of a virgin; was a prophet and apostle of God; was to be revered and held in high regard; was a wise teacher; was a miracle worker; ascended into Heaven in bodily form; will sit beside Allah during the judgment; and will come again as a follower of Muhammad to revive Islam. Muslims either deny that Jesus was crucified or that He died on the cross. Many simply believe Jesus' death was an illusion.

Of all the teachings of Christianity, no doctrine is more imperative than the bodily resurrection of Jesus Christ from the dead. The truth of the resurrection has been attacked from every angle. New books and television media regularly appear questioning the resurrection, re-hashing old theories about what happened to Jesus' body. Since resurrection is crucial to Christianity, we will take a scientific approach to examine it.

The encyclopedia describes the **Scientific method** as a body of techniques for investigating phenomena and acquiring new knowledge, as well as for correcting and integrating previous knowledge. It is based on gathering observable, empirical, measurable evidence, subject to specific principles of reasoning. In this chapter, we are going to use the Scientific method to examine the central truth of Christianity. Is the Resurrection of Christ fact or fiction?

A student at the University of Uruguay asked **Josh McDowell**, a well-known defender of Christianity, "*Professor McDowell, why can't you refute Christianity?*"

"*For a very simple reason,*" McDowell answered. "*I am not able to explain away an event in history--the resurrection of Jesus Christ.*" The resurrection of Jesus Christ is either one of the most wicked, vicious, heartless hoaxes ever foisted on the minds of human beings--or it is the most remarkable fact of history.

Christianity has many extraordinary claims, but they all rest on this one event, the resurrection of our Lord. If this event did not come to pass, Christianity would be of no use. The Bible in **1 Corinthians 15:14** says, "*And if Christ has not been raised, our preaching is useless and so is your faith.*"

Here is some of the background information relevant to the resurrection: Jesus of Nazareth, a Jewish prophet who claimed to be the Christ prophesied in the Jewish Scriptures, was arrested, judged a political criminal, and crucified. Three days after His death and burial, some women who went to His tomb found the body gone. In subsequent weeks, His disciples claimed that God had raised Him from the dead and that He appeared to them various times before ascending into heaven.

From that foundation, Christianity spread throughout the Roman Empire and has continued to exert great influence through the centuries.

E. M. Blaiklock, Professor of Classics at Auckland University, stated, *"I claim to be a historian. My approach to Classics is historical. And I tell you that the evidence for the life, the death, and the resurrection of Christ is better authenticated than most of the facts of ancient history,"*

Professor **Thomas Arnold**, for 14 years a headmaster of Rugby, England, author of the famous "History of Rome" and appointed to the chair of modern history at Oxford University, was well acquainted with the value of evidence in determining historical facts. This great scholar said, *"I have been used for many years to study the histories of other times and to examine and weigh the evidence of those who have written about them, and I know of no one fact in the history of mankind which is proved by better and fuller evidence of every sort, to the understanding of a fair inquirer, than the great sign which God hath given us that Christ died and rose again from the dead."*

Brooke Foss Westcott, an English scholar, said: *"Taking all the evidence together, it is not too much to say that there is no historic incident better or more variously supported than the resurrection of Christ. Nothing but the antecedent assumption that it must be false could have suggested the idea of deficiency in the proof of it."*

Let's briefly investigate a few of the numerous pieces of evidence and proofs supporting the facts of the Death and Resurrection of Jesus.

CHRIST DIED - In 1986, **The American Medical Association** published an article titled "*The Physical Death of Jesus Christ.*" It details the entire process of Jesus' trial to His death on the cross. In **Luke 22**, before Jesus is arrested, it is written that He was in great distress and sweating blood. Although rare, it is recognized as Hematidrosis, caused by high amounts of stress.

At the time, the crucifixion was considered the worst death for the worst of criminals. But this is not all Jesus faced. He endured whipping so severely that it tore the flesh from His body. He was beaten so horrifically that His face was torn, and His beard ripped. A crown of thorns, 2–3 inches long, cut deeply into His scalp. The leather whip used to flog Him had tiny iron balls and sharp bones. The balls caused internal injuries while the sharp bones ripped open His flesh. His skeletal muscles, veins, and bowels were exposed, causing major blood loss. Most men do not survive this kind of torture. After Jesus was severely flogged, He was forced to carry His own cross while people mocked and spat on Him.

Crucifixion was a process meant to instill excruciating pain, creating a slow and agonizing death. Nails as long as 8 inches were driven into Jesus' wrists and feet. The Roman soldiers knew the tendon in the wrists would tear and break, forcing Jesus to use His back muscles to support Himself to breathe. Imagine the struggle and the pain Jesus endured for three hours!

John 19:33-34 records that after Jesus' death, a Roman soldier pierced His side with a spear, and blood and water came out. Scientists explain that from hypovolemic shock, the rapid heart rate causes fluid to gather in the sack around the lungs and heart. The gathering of fluid in the membrane around the heart is called Pericardial effusion, and in the lungs, Pleural effusion. The fluid was flowing from the pericardium, the lining around the wall of the heart, where a heart rupture causes a division of a blood clot and a watery serum. Christ could not have survived this spearing but most likely had already died. The collapsing lungs, failing heart, dehydration, and inability to get sufficient oxygen to the tissues essentially suffocated Jesus. The decreased oxygen also damages the heart itself (myocardial infarction), which leads to cardiac arrest and rupture in severe cases. Jesus most likely died of a heart attack.

EMPTY TOMB - After viewing the empty tomb, the disciples of Christ went right back to the city of Jerusalem, where, if what they were teaching was false, the falsity would be evident. The empty tomb was "too notorious to be denied." The resurrection "could not have been maintained in Jerusalem for a single day, for a single hour, if the emptiness of the tomb had not been established as a fact for all concerned - both friend and enemy.

GRAVECLOTHES – John and Peter, disciples of Jesus, looked over to the place where the body of Jesus had lain, and there were the grave clothes, in the form of the body.

JESUS' APPEARANCES AFTER RESURRECTION CONFIRMED - Over 500 witnesses physically saw Jesus during the forty days after His resurrection (**1 Corinthians 15:6**). In a court of law, one eyewitness usually is sufficient to confirm a fact; 500 eyewitnesses would be overwhelming proof. The resurrection of Jesus was also declared in numerous other accounts, including the appearance of Jesus to Mary

Magdalene (**John 20:10-18**), to other women (**Matthew 28:8-10**), to Cleopas and his companion (**Luke 24:13-32**), to eleven disciples and others (**Luke 24:33-49**), to ten apostles and others (excluding Thomas) (**John 20:19-23**), to the apostles (including Thomas) (**John 20:26-30**), to seven apostles (**John 21:1-14**), to the disciples (**Matthew 28:16-20**), and to the apostles on the Mount of Olives (**Luke 24:50-52** and **Acts 1:4-9**).

HOSTILE WITNESSES - There was certainly a plethora of hostile witnesses to the events of the Gospels, but not a single Roman came forward to expose supposed fallacies. Many Roman critics attacked the philosophy of Christianity, but they were unable to attack its historical accuracy, as they were witnesses to the events of the New Testament. The Church could not have grown in Jerusalem if Jesus' own generation (who had Him put to death) could have immediately exposed the resurrection as lies.

In addition, no author or informed individual would regard Saul of Tarsus as being a follower of Christ. The facts show the exact opposite. Saul despised Christ and persecuted Christ's followers. It was a life-shattering experience when Christ appeared to him. (**Acts 9**) Although he was at the time not a disciple, he later became the apostle Paul, one of the greatest witnesses to the truth of the resurrection. Paul's experience caused him to immediately change from a nasty persecutor of Christianity to one of its most aggressive advocates. He claimed that this change came only after personally interacting with the resurrected Christ, and he willingly suffered and died for his testimony.

JESUS' EARLY FOLLOWERS SUFFER AND DIE FOR THEIR TESTIMONY - This established fact attests to the sincerity of their faith and strongly rules out deception on their part. In fact, all but one of the

New Testament's writers was executed for proclaiming and defending Christ's resurrection (John alone was spared but forced into exile by the Roman Emperor Titus Flavius Domitianus). This is truly compelling evidence of the resurrection.

Granted, martyrdom is not unique -- many throughout history have willingly died for their beliefs. What makes the disciples' martyrdom extraordinary to me is that these men were able to know whether what they were professing was true. You see, no one will knowingly suffer horribly and ultimately die a brutal death to defend something they know to be a lie. They had nothing to gain from lying and, obviously, everything to lose.

HISTORICAL AUTHORITIES OUTSIDE THE BIBLE DOCUMENT THE RESURRECTION AND PERSECUTION – These include Josephus, a prominent Jewish historian; Tacitus, a Roman historian; John Foxe, the Greek satirist, and others including Gaius Suetonius Tranquillas, Flavius Josephus, Thallus, Pliny the younger, Justin Martyr, Tertullian, and the Jewish Sanhedrin.

STATEMENT ON THE RESURRECTION BY CHUCK COLSON (former White House special counsel to Richard Nixon, who was sent to prison for his role in the early 1970s Watergate cover-up) *"I know the resurrection is a fact, and Watergate proved it to me. How? Because twelve men testified, they had seen Jesus raised from the dead, then they proclaimed that truth for forty years, never once denying it. Everyone was beaten, tortured, stoned, and put in prison. They would not have endured that if it weren't true. Watergate embroiled twelve of the most powerful men in the world, and they couldn't keep a lie for three weeks. You're telling me twelve apostles could keep a lie for forty years? Absolutely impossible."*

ATTEMPTS TO PROVE THAT THE RESURRECTION IS FICTION HAVE FAILED

Among these are the following three:

Simon Greenleaf (1783-1853) was one of the founders of Harvard Law School. He authored the authoritative three-volume text, *A Treatise on the Law of Evidence* (1842), which is still considered the greatest single authority on evidence in the entire literature of legal procedure. Greenleaf literally wrote the rules of evidence for the U.S. legal system. He was certainly a man who knew how to weigh the facts. He was an atheist until he accepted a challenge from his students to investigate the case of Christ's resurrection. After personally collecting and examining the evidence based on rules of evidence that he helped establish, Greenleaf became a Christian and wrote the classic "*Testimony of the Evangelists.*"

Sir Lionel Luckhoo (1914-1997) is considered one of the greatest lawyers in British history. He has been recorded in the *Guinness Book of World Records* as the "World's Most Successful Advocate," with 245 consecutive murder acquittals. He was knighted by Queen Elizabeth II—twice. Luckhoo declared, "*I humbly add I have spent more than forty-two years as a defense trial lawyer appearing in many parts of the world and am still in active practice. I have been fortunate to secure a number of successes in jury trials, and I say unequivocally the evidence for the Resurrection of Jesus Christ is so overwhelming that it compels acceptance by proof which leaves absolutely no room for doubt.*"

Lee Strobel was a Yale-educated, award-winning journalist at the Chicago Tribune. As an atheist, he decided to compile a legal case against Jesus Christ and prove him to be a fraud by the weight of the evidence. As Legal Editor of the Tribune, Strobel's area of expertise was courtroom analysis. Remarkably, after compiling and critically examining the evidence for himself, Strobel became a Christian. Stunned by his findings, he organized the evidence into a book entitled *"The Case for Christ,"* which won the Gold Medallion Book Award for excellence.

People all over the world have the choice to accept or reject Jesus and His Death and Resurrection based on their own convictions. If they choose to deny the fact of Jesus, His Death, and His Resurrection, it is not for a lack of witnesses nor a lack of evidence.

To the world, Christianity is as foolish as it can get. They believe it's for the weak. But when you are confronted by the reality of the cross, it's clearly not a pretty sight. It is brutal and horrific. This is the weight Jesus carried. The weight of the sins of the world, all so that we can live. God's wrath is fully satisfied in Jesus. This is what it took.

"I have been crucified with Christ and I no longer live, but Christ lives in me. The life I now live in the body, I live by faith in the Son of God, who loved me and gave Himself for me" (**Galatians 2:20**).

SOME PERSONAL STEPS IN SHOE LEATHER

Several years ago, I first presented this Resurrection of Jesus truth to a classroom of college students in Venezuela, which resulted in changing many of their skeptical hearts. Only God knows how He used those students thereafter, but I am sure it was for His glory in a nation that is currently in economic and political chaos.

Recently I watched the movie "The Case for Christ," which provided me the reality that many people just simply refuse to believe in Christ's resurrection even though the evidence is overwhelming. We live in a time where truth is denied and becomes relative, which allows people *"to do what is right in their own eyes."*

The **Good News and Truth** to me and all other believers is that **Jesus was resurrected** so that through Him, we can have "**new life**" with Him eternally.

CHAPTER 4.
PURPOSE OF OUR LIFE JOURNEY

"Without God, life has no purpose, and without purpose, life has no meaning. Without meaning, life has no significance or hope." — **Rick Warren,** American pastor and author of "The Purpose Driven Life."

Ephesians 2:8–9 is an extremely popular passage of Scripture about salvation by grace (undeserved and unconditional love)— *"For by grace are you saved through faith in Christ and that is not of yourselves, it is the gift from God. Not of works, lest any man should boast."* These two verses are so often quoted, and many miss out on **verse 10,** which offers tremendous insight into what God desires after salvation from the penalty of sin.

God in **Ephesians 2:10** gives a personal message for His children concerning their purpose for their life journey— *"We are His workmanship created in Christ Jesus for good works, which God prepared beforehand so that we would walk in them."* We are crafted, with skill and creativity, by God, for His purposes.

Interestingly, God prepared what He wanted us to do for Him long ago. He has already planned for what He wants us to do with our lives. God calls all Christian believers to be involved in some common purposes that apply to all of us. However, He has a unique plan for each of us to serve Him in this world. In our created uniqueness, we do not need to copy what someone else has done or is doing.

God indwells us with His Holy Spirit to provide the power to lead us in our service to Him. The Holy Spirit also provides each of His children with certain unique spiritual gifts (discussed in Chapter 5) of His sovereign choosing to do His purpose.

GOD'S COMMON PURPOSES FOR ALL BELIEVERS

Many of the common purposes in which God wants all His children involved are closely related and overlapping; they include:

(1) Be conformed to the Image of Christ.

God's purpose in creation and redemption is to have a family of children conformed to the image of His Son. Jesus is our identity, and He, through His indwelling Holy Spirit, lives His life through us, so our chief purpose in this life is to be like Him. In our daily walk with Jesus, we learn from Him, and His Spirit is helping us do His will over our own will. Thus, we are becoming more like Jesus.

"But God has not called us to be like those around us. He has called us to be like Himself. Holiness is nothing less than the conformity to the character of God." —**Jerry Bridges,** author of "The Pursuit of Happiness"

(2) Bring God glory.

1 Corinthians 10:31 tells us, *"….in whatever you do, do it all for the glory of God."* In fact, God tells us in **Isaiah 43:7** that He created us for His glory. *"Let your light shine before others, so that they may see your good works and give glory to your Father who is in Heaven."* (**Matthew 5:16**)

We often want God to be our life coach rather than our Lord. We want three to five helpful tips on how to live an easier or more pleasure-filled life. We want maximum freedom for ourselves, but we want His controlling interventions when something goes wrong. It is always about us. We forget that our comfort is not our end. His glory is our goal.

To glorify God is to mirror His image, which is to love, and love generously, as He does. Also, to extol His attributes, praise His works, trust His name, and obey His Word.

In the refrain of her 1875 hymn, "To God Be The Glory," **Fanny Crosby** exhorts us to do what is right by extolling the Lord for all His work: *"O come to the Father through Jesus the Son and give Him the glory, great things He has done!"*

(3) Love God and love others.

Jesus, in **Matthew 22:36–40,** was asked the question, *"Which is the greatest commandment in the law?"* He answered, *"You shall love the Lord your God with all of your heart, soul, strength, and mind; this is the first and great commandment. And the second is like it, love your neighbor as yourself. These two summarize all the law and the prophets."*

Love always involves a relationship. Love involves more than emotion; it focuses on our positive actions for others without taking ourselves into consideration.

"Beloved, let us love one another, for love is from God and whoever loves has been born of God and knows God. Anyone who does not love does not know God because God is love." (**1 John 4:7–21**)

Our love needs to have an eternal perspective primarily and a temporal perspective secondarily. Love that provides temporary earthly needs and services is definitely good and Christlike but should have as its ultimate Christlike goal of being used by God in His eternal redemptive plan for the souls of men and women.

"Do you know that nothing you do in this life will ever matter, unless it is about loving God and loving the people he has made?" — **Francis Chan**, American author, and pastor

(4) Be Witnesses for Christ.

The second greatest commandment of loving your neighbor as yourself was highlighted by Jesus forty days after His resurrection. The last thing that Jesus Christ said to His disciples before ascending into heaven was the one and most important thing that He wanted them to remember. He had been teaching and training them for three years and could have chosen to remind them of any one of a thousand lessons, or He could have summarized His ministry so it would be very clear in their minds. However, He chose **Acts 1:8,** where He states, *"You will receive power when the Holy Spirit has come upon you; and you shall be My witnesses both in Jerusalem, and in all Judea and Samaria, and even to the remotest part of the earth."*

Jesus basically commissions all of Jesus' disciples, including future ones, with the job of telling others about Jesus. It has two parts to it—the disciples' responsibility or job and God's provision to help them do that job. It is called the Great Commission and is the shoe leather proof of loving your neighbor as yourself.

In essence, proof of loving someone as yourself is sharing with them the salvation and eternal life that is available through Christ. We will look at this in-depth in the chapter "Bragging on Jesus."

(5) Trust God and His Sovereignty.

Romans 1:17, Galatians 3:11, and **Hebrews 10:38** all tell us to *"live by faith,"*—meaning that we believe and trust God even when we can't see Him or understand His sovereign ways.

For God to have sovereignty means that He has the absolute right to do all things because He alone has all power and all knowledge. God is in control of all things, yet at times He may choose to let certain events happen according to natural laws which He has ordained, including the consequences for sin and fallen nature. If there is any element of the universe that is outside of His authority, then He no longer is God over all creation.

While God has power over all things and knowledge of all things, He still gives us freedom within His sovereignty. We are neither the authors nor the pawns of our life stories, but rather we are given freedom within God's will to make decisions, yet all our circumstances are under God's providence and power.

"I think to trust in the sovereignty of God does not excuse my personal responsibility. Just the opposite—it equips me to be personally responsible." — **Max Lucado,** American author and pastor

God's plan leaves room for our choices, and if we know what He expects to happen, or at least that He has a plan, it is less distressing when things do not go according to our plan. We have the freedom to move, knowing that God's plan might supersede ours, but that is because His plan is based less on whims and more on knowing the big picture.

Though God's sovereignty can be initially hard to accept, ultimately, it is the only solid ground to stand on in this broken world. His sovereign power to redeem the suffering we experience in this sin-ridden world is our only true hope and comfort. Without confidence in God's sovereign oversight of the universe, life becomes meaningless, hope for justice fades, and everything seems random. The truth is, if God is not sovereign, then we're in trouble. The sovereignty of God is a rock underfoot when the winds blow in our lives. It confronts what seems absurd in our existence. God's sovereignty is our greatest hope as we face an uncertain and unknown future.

God was willing to give His Son for your soul. He values you. He knows all the details and plans for your life. He loves you! He is sovereign. Trust Him.

(6) Be Thankful to God in Everything.

1 Thessalonians 5:18 *"In everything give thanks; for this is the will of God in Christ Jesus concerning you."* When we allow ourselves to have a negative mindset and focus on things and situations that displease us, our minds become darkened. We can shine light into that darkness by thanking God even though we may not feel thankful. We can always walk in the light by practicing the discipline of thanksgiving, knowing that God is in control.

"God is in control, and therefore in everything I can give thanks – not because of the situation but because of the One who directs and rules over it." — **Kay Arthur,** Bible teacher and author

(7) Pray.

"Pray without ceasing." (**1 Thessalonians 5:17**) Prayer is our lifeline to God. Recognizing the reality of the presence of God is to have an open line of communication with Him in everything. It is amazing that the Creator God desires this intimate continuous contact with each of His children.

"Prayer is the greatest of all forces, because it honors God and brings Him into active aid." — **E. M. Bounds**, American author of nine books on prayer

GOD'S SPECIFIC PLANS AND PURPOSE

Proverbs 3:5–6 tells us, *"Trust in the Lord with all your heart and lean not on your own understanding. In all your ways acknowledge Him, and He shall direct your paths."*

The powerful hand that upholds all things and directs our paths is the hand that was pierced for us. Jesus Christ came to save our souls and get us back on God's plan. The death and resurrection of Christ invite us to trust Him with our lives. When we see Christ as God, there is a deep comfort in knowing that He sees what we cannot see and that He has purposes greater than any of our plans.

We rejoice when we read in **Jeremiah 29:11,** *"For I know the plans I have for you," declares the Lord, plans to prosper you and not to harm you, plans to give you hope and a future."* This verse primarily was a promise by our Sovereign God to a group of people going through a tough time who would likely all die as slaves. It is a promise that God is still in control even when things are bleak. It's a promise that even though things might not make sense to them now, God's plan is still good. It is giving hope to people that are struggling with understanding what God is doing. This verse is applicable to us today and provides some comfortable shoe leather as we walk through a fallen world.

Many of God's plans are detailed throughout the Bible. He has plans for nations, for people groups, and for individuals. **Isaiah 46:10–11** summarizes what God wants us to know about His plans: *"My purpose will stand, and I will do all that I please. From the east I summon a bird of prey; from a far-off land, a man to fulfill my purpose. What I have said, that I will bring about; what I have planned, that I will do."* It's one thing to recognize that God has an overarching plan for the world; it is quite another to acknowledge that God has a specific life plan for each person.

Many places in Scripture indicate that God does have a specific plan for each human being. It starts before we are conceived. The Lord told Jeremiah, *"Before I formed you in the womb I knew you, before you were born I set you apart; I appointed you as a prophet to the nations"* **(Jeremiah 1:5).** God's plan was not reactive, a response to Jeremiah's conception. It was preemptive, implying that God specially formed this male child to accomplish His plan. David underscores this truth: *"You created my inmost being; You knit me together in my mother's womb"* **(Psalm 139:13).** Unborn children are not accidents. They are being formed by their Creator for His purposes.

As it is in any biological family, babies are mainly "takers" who must be fed, clothed, washed, etc., and are, for the most part, unable to do for themselves. The babies are self-centered. The parents must be the "givers" to babies. It is only when babies grow up that they begin to do things for themselves and be mature enough to be trained and taught to do for others.

So, until they grow up, spiritual babies focus on and serve only themselves. God, in most cases, does not begin to use babies for their unique purpose until they grow up spiritually, which in most cases takes years of spiritual nourishment and training in God's Word. It is virtually impossible to grow spiritually without eating and drinking God's Word.

A sad fact exists that many Christians in the family of God cannot be used effectively for the purposes of God because they remain babies and never grow up spiritually. As spiritual babies grow up and mature, they begin to be used by God in His general common purposes previously talked about in this chapter and begin to have opportunities where God begins slowly to reveal His unique purposes for them.

It is difficult to be used for a specific purpose until we are actively involved in the common purposes. As we journey through life striving to do God's common purposes for our lives, His specific plans and purpose unfold naturally as we grow in faith, mature in knowledge, and practice obedience with all we understand. As we obey His common plans for all His children, we begin to discover His uniquely designed plan and purpose for us individually.

As we walk in His shoe leather, we discover our own spiritual gifts and abilities (see Chapter 5) that specially suit us to serve Him in unique ways

(**1 Corinthians 12: 4–11**). Instead of letting His glory shape our desires and ambitions, we too often expect Him to reveal His minute-by-minute instructions for our lives. We expect Him to spell out everything. We crave the personal comfort of knowing our destined five-year plan instead of faithfully trusting Him for the next five years.

Even when we have been spiritually nourished and are growing through His Word, we have a tendency to become impatient in wondering what God's plan is for our lives. But it is not as complicated as we make it out to be. God's plan for us is revealed a little at a time as we follow Him, and His plan may look different in different seasons of life. God's plan is rarely a straight shot to a visible goal. His plan requires of us a journey, and that journey may be filled with detours, sudden stops, and confusing turns. But if our hearts are set to obey Him in all that we know to do, then we will be in the center of His will every step of the way.

In different parts of growing up, these purposes can appear to change. We forget that faith might look messy and that we might not have our entire life plan unveiled to us immediately. Sometimes, we must step forward with both confidence and uncertainty. We forget that while God has conquered death through his Son on the cross, we still live in a fallen world and are amid a spiritual war between good and evil.

We forget that He's sovereign over us. Abraham and Sarah had to wait twenty-five years for God to fulfill His promise of an heir to make him a great nation; Joseph had to wait thirteen years for God's purpose to be fulfilled after being sold into slavery by his brothers to become the second most powerful man in Egypt. Moses, Caleb, and Joshua wandered in the wilderness for forty years waiting on God's promise. Jesus waited thirty years before He began His public ministry.

There are numerous other examples in the Bible where God's timing was perfect, and the person was spiritually equipped to accomplish God's ultimate purpose. However, as we read in the Bible, God certainly used these persons in different ways to bring Him glory while waiting. God has not changed; He still uses His children in many ways to bring Him glory, even before using them for their specific purposes.

Through the power of the Holy Spirit, God transforms us (**2 Corinthians 3:18**). As we keep our prayerful focus on God through His Word and doing His common purposes, He will do His creative sanctification work in us and form us into the disciples that He sovereignly wants us to be with special purposes. This process is on God's timetable, and we cannot speed it up. God wants to sovereignly use His children in the best ways possible for His glory. God does not play hide and seek with His specific purposes. We do not have to do assessments and testing to find these. **God, in His timing, will provide the passion and the opportunities for which He has trained and taught us so long as we continue to step out in faith and obedience.**

However, the freedom of choice that God allows His children will many times result in our quenching (extinguishing the fire) the Holy Spirit and ignoring the opportunities to be involved with our specific purposes.

Yes, it is possible for a believer to miss God's specific will/purpose for his/her life as it is for a believer to choose to ignore or minimize the common purposes.

As was mentioned before, the sad fact is that many believers, who have accepted Christ as their savior and have been born again, never grow from being spiritual babies because they have never chosen the necessary nourishment of an **intense prayerful diet of the Word of God**. As a result, they could miss God's common purposes and specific purposes for their earthly lives.

"It was becoming clearer and clearer that if I wanted to come to the end of my life and not say, 'I've wasted it!' then I would need to press all the way in, and all the way up, to the ultimate purpose of God and join him in it. If my life was to have a single, all-satisfying, unifying passion, it would have to be God's passion." — **John Piper,** American theologian.

SOME PERSONAL STEPS IN SHOE LEATHER

As I remember back in my own personal life, what I would have seen as God's purpose for my life in high school drastically changed in college and then again in my first years in the workplace and marriage. Because God opened doors for my playing college football, it appeared that He would use me in professional sports in some way. I had received a letter from Vince Lombardi, the renowned coach of the Green Bay Packers, saying that they planned to draft me in the future. A neck injury requiring surgery put a halt to that possibility. Also, I was the number two person in rank in the advanced Reserved Officers Training Corps (ROTC) while in college and thought that God might use me in the military, but I could not pass my military physical exam to get my officer's commission because of my neck injury. Five years of employment with a major oil company involving extensive travel and moving living locations four times certainly added minimal insight into God's purpose.

It was only after becoming a partner in private business did God begin to "whet my appetite" for the Bible. Spending more and more time in God's Word accelerated my spiritual growth from being a baby to a maturing disciple of Christ. Now God, in His timing, was ready to use me for His unique purposes.

God instilled in me a hunger for the Word of God, which led to in-depth study and wanting to share what I was learning with others. The Holy Spirit's spiritual gift of teaching became very evident, for which He used me for over forty years to teach home, church, and business Bible studies. Also, God, during those years, provided multiple opportunities to start and/or lead various ministries, which are listed in "About The Author" in this book.

At the same time, God has had me focused on secular businesses from which He provides financial resources for His spiritual gift of giving to help accelerate the Great Commission. In addition, He now has me using my Bible knowledge and teaching to write books to bring God glory as I continue, along with my two sons, in a family business. Over the years, it has become clear that **through the power of the Holy Spirit**, I have become an entrepreneur of God in the marketplace and around the world.

CHAPTER 5.
OUR EVER-PRESENT
TRAVELING COMPANION

"If you know Christ, you don't need to beg for the Holy Spirit to come into your life; He is already there—whether you feel His presence or not. Don't confuse the Holy Spirit with an emotional feeling or a particular type of spiritual experience." — **Billy Graham**

Jesus, on the night before He was crucified on the cross, was informing His disciples that He was getting ready to leave them after being their traveling companion for three years while *discipling* them. In **John 16:7,** Jesus tells them, *"Nevertheless, I tell you the truth: it is to your advantage that I go away, for if I do not go away, the Helper (Advocate, Comforter, Counselor) will not come to you. But if I go, I will send Him to you."*

This statement would have been difficult for His disciples to understand. The suggestion that Jesus was leaving and that would be beneficial to them would be almost impossible for them to grasp.

So long as Jesus is there, in person, the object of the disciples' faith will always be a physical person whom they can touch and see. As was true in their three years of journeying with Jesus, they would constantly depend on Him to direct, train, and teach them and answer their questions. Their own thoughts and conscience would consistently be dismissed in favor of asking Jesus for His thoughts and truths. When He would not be there, they would feel incomplete.

It is obvious that Jesus, in His physical body, was limited on how many places He could be and on how many people with whom He could be intimately involved. The Holy Spirit (Helper, Advocate, Comforter, Counselor) has no such limits and is omnipresent in all believers.

In **Matthew 28:20,** Jesus makes this remarkable statement before ascending into Heaven after His resurrection, "I am with you always." The Holy Spirit provides the way for each Christian believer to have personal, intimate, and continuous contact with God, who indwells each of them. They have an ever-present traveling companion everywhere they go.

Most Christians accept this teaching as truth but ignore it in daily living. A few believers center their lives around this reality and truly live abundant lives, blessed beyond all expectations.

The intent of this chapter is to learn the wonderful truths about the Holy Spirit so that all of us can live abundantly in the reality of His presence in our lives.

Trinity of God

It is impossible to understand the Bible, Christian living, the structure of the church, or our own relationship with God without recognizing the Trinity—Father, Son, and Holy Spirit.

The **Christian concept of the Trinity** is difficult to comprehend perfectly and completely. It is challenging for any human being to fully perceive, let alone explain. God is infinitely greater than we are; therefore, we should not expect to be able to fully understand Him. The Bible teaches that the Father is God, that Jesus is God, and that the Holy Spirit is God. The Bible also teaches that there is only one God. Though we can understand some facts about the relationship of the different Persons of the Trinity to one another, ultimately, it is hard to grasp mentally.

"Bring me a worm that can comprehend a man, and then I will show you a man that can comprehend the Triune God." — **John Wesley,** English theologian and evangelist

However, this does not mean the Trinity is not true or that it is not based on the teachings of the Bible. The Trinity is one God existing in three Persons. Understand that this is not in any way suggesting three Gods. The Trinity is not one plus one plus one equals three; it is one times one times one equals one. Keep in mind when studying this subject that the word "Trinity" is not found in Scripture. This is a term that is used to attempt to describe the triune God—three coexistent, co-eternal Persons who are God. Of real importance is that the concept represented by the word "Trinity" does exist in Scripture.

The following is what God's Word says about the Trinity:

1. <u>**There is one God**</u> (Deuteronomy 6:4; 1 Corinthians 8:4; Galatians 3:20; 1 Timothy 2:5).

2. <u>**The Trinity consists of three Persons**</u> (Genesis 1:1, 26; 3:22; 11:7; Isaiah 6:8, 48:16, 61:1; Matthew 3:16–17, 28:19; 2 Corinthians 13:14). In **Genesis 1:1,** the Hebrew plural noun "Elohim" is used. In **Genesis 1:26, 3:22, 11:7,** and **Isaiah 6:8,** the plural pronoun for "us" is used. The word "Elohim" and the pronoun "us" are plural forms, definitely referring in the Hebrew language to more than two. While this is not an explicit argument for the Trinity, it does denote the aspect of plurality in God. The Hebrew word for "God," "Elohim," definitely allows for the Trinity.

    In **Isaiah 48:16** and **61:1**, the Son is speaking while referring to the Father and the Holy Spirit. Compare **Isaiah 61:1** to **Luke 4:14–19** to see that it is the Son speaking. **Matthew 3:16–17** describes the event of Jesus' baptism. Seen in this passage is God the Holy Spirit descending on God the Son while God the Father proclaims His pleasure in the Son.

    Matthew 28:19 and **2 Corinthians 13:14** are other examples of passages that present three distinct Persons in the Trinity.

3. <u>**The members of the Trinity are distinguished from one another in various passages.**</u> In the Old Testament, the "LORD" is distinguished from the "Lord" (**Genesis 19:24; Hosea 1:4**). The LORD has a Son (**Psalm 2:7, 12; Proverbs 30:2–4**). The Spirit is distinguished from the "LORD" (**Numbers 27:18**) and from "God" (**Psalm 51:10–12**).

God the Son is distinguished from God the Father (**Psalm 45:6–7; Hebrews 1:8–9**). In the New Testament, Jesus speaks to the Father about sending a Helper, the Holy Spirit (**John 14:16–17**). This shows that Jesus did not consider Himself to be the Father or the Holy Spirit. Also, consider the other instances when Jesus speaks to the Father. Was He speaking to Himself? No. He spoke to another Person in the Trinity—the Father.

4. **Each member of the Trinity is God.** The Father is God (**John 6:27; Romans 1:7; 1 Peter 1:2**). The Son is God (**John 1:1, 14; Romans 9:5; Colossians 2:9; Hebrews 1:8; 1 John 5:20**). The Holy Spirit is God (**Acts 5:3–4; 1 Corinthians 3:16**).

5. **The individual members of the Trinity have different tasks.** The Father is the ultimate source or cause of the universe (**1 Corinthians 8:6; Revelation 4:11**); divine revelation (**Revelation 1:1**); salvation (**John 3:16–17**); and Jesus' human works (**John 5:17; 14:10**). The Father initiates all of these things.

The Son is the agent through whom the Father does the following works: the creation and maintenance of the universe (**1 Corinthians 8:6; John 1:3; Colossians 1:16–17**); divine revelation (**John 1:1, 16:12–15; Matthew 11:27; Revelation 1:1**); and salvation (**2 Corinthians 5:19; Matthew 1:21; John 4:42**). The Father does all these things through the Son, who functions as His agent.

The Holy Spirit is the means by whom the Father does the following works: creation and maintenance of the universe (**Genesis 1:2; Job 26:13; Psalm 104:30**); divine revelation (**John 16:12–15; Ephesians 3:5; 2 Peter 1:21**); salvation (**John 3:6; Titus 3:5; 1 Peter 1:2**); and

Jesus' works (**Isaiah 61:1; Acts 10:38**). Thus, the Father does all these things by the power of the Holy Spirit.

In addition, in **Ephesians 1:3–14,** Paul describes the roles of God (Father), Jesus Christ, and the Holy Spirit in this beautiful passage.

There have been many attempts to develop illustrations of the Trinity. However, none of the popular illustrations are completely accurate. The egg and apple fail in that the shell, white, and yolk are parts of the egg, not the egg in themselves, just as the skin, flesh, and seeds of the apple are parts of it, not the apple itself. The Father, Son, and Holy Spirit are not parts of God; each of them is God. The water illustration is somewhat better, but it still fails to adequately describe the Trinity. Liquid, vapor, and ice are forms of water. The Father, Son, and Holy Spirit are not forms of God; each of them is God. So, while these illustrations may give us a picture of the Trinity, the picture is not entirely accurate. An infinite God cannot be fully described by a finite illustration.

The doctrine of the Trinity has been a divisive issue throughout the entire history of the Christian church. While the core aspects of the Trinity are clearly presented in God's Word, some of the side issues are not as explicitly clear. **The Father is God, the Son is God, and the Holy Spirit is God— but there is only one God. That is the biblical doctrine of the Trinity.**

The Holy Spirit

He is probably the least understood person of the Trinity. He is invisible but real. The Holy Spirit is not an "it"; He is a person.

"If we think of the Holy Spirit only as an impersonal power or influence, then our thought will constantly be, how can I get hold of and use the Holy Spirit? But if we think of Him in the biblical way as a divine Person, infinitely wise, infinitely holy, infinitely tender, then our thought will constantly be, 'How can the Holy Spirit get hold of and use me?" — **R. A. Torrey,** American evangelist

Being a person, the <u>Holy Spirit</u> has feelings. He can become sad or angry, and others can insult Him and blaspheme against Him.

"Yet they rebelled and grieved His Holy Spirit. So, He turned and became their enemy and He himself fought against them" **(Isaiah 63:10)**.

"And so, I tell you, every kind of sin and slander can be forgiven, but blasphemy against the Spirit will not be forgiven" **(Matthew 12:31)**.

"You stiff-necked people! Your hearts and ears are still uncircumcised. You are just like your ancestors: You always resist the Holy Spirit!" **(Acts 7:51)**.

"And do not grieve the Holy Spirit of God, with whom you were sealed for the day of redemption" **(Ephesians 4:30)**.

He has intentions, shows willfulness and discretion, loves, communicates, testifies, teaches, and prays. These are qualities that distinguish Him as a person.

"You gave your good Spirit to instruct them…" **(Nehemiah 9:20)**.

"When the Advocate comes, whom I will send to you from the Father—the Spirit of truth who goes out from the Father—he will testify about me" **(John 15:26)**.

"While they were worshiping the Lord and fasting, the Holy Spirit said, "Set apart for me Barnabas and Saul for the work to which I have called them" (**Acts 13:2**).

"In the same way, the Spirit helps us in our weakness. We do not know what we ought to pray for, but the Spirit himself intercedes for us through wordless groans. And he who searches our hearts knows the mind of the Spirit, because the Spirit intercedes for God's people in accordance with the will of God" (**Romans 8:26–27**).

"All these are the work of one and the same Spirit, and he distributes them to each one, just as he determines" (**1 Corinthians 12:11**).

Each of these preceding emotions and acts are characteristics of a person. The Holy Spirit is not an impersonal force, like gravity or magnetism or the Star Wars "force." He is a person with all the attributes of personality.

The Holy Spirit is God present in the lives of believers, and He works in various ways.

1.   Convicts the World of Sin

"Nevertheless, I tell you the truth: it is to your advantage that I go away, for if I do not go away, the Helper will not come to you. But if I go, I will send him to you. And when he comes, he will convict the world concerning sin and righteousness and judgment" (**John 16:7–8**).

Conviction is not the same as conversion. It is convincing or refuting an opponent so that he has the matter set before him in a clear light, whether he accepts or rejects the evidence. Conviction, then, offers proof but does not guarantee the truth will be accepted, which is necessary for conversion. The order of conviction is a logical one. Man needs to see his state of sin, have proof of righteousness that only the Savior provides, and be reminded that if the person refuses to receive the Savior, he will face condemnation. The ways that the Holy Spirit convicts include speaking directly to the man's mind and conscience, speaking through the written or audio Word of God, and using the spoken testimony or preached Word.

2. Gives New Life

Ephesians 2:1 reports that we are dead in our sins. Our human spirit within us, made in the image of God, is dead toward God. Mankind needs life. Yet, we have all sinned and, therefore, are dead toward God.

The Holy Spirit, however, gives us new life in Jesus Christ. Jesus said, "*No one can see the Kingdom of God unless they are born again*" (**John 3:3**). But how is someone born again? What does that mean? The Holy Spirit is the one who makes you born again; it is a supernatural act. "*He saved us, not because of the righteous things we have done, but because of His mercy. He washed away our sins, giving us a new birth and new life through the Holy Spirit.*" (**Titus 3:5**). All we must do is accept the free gift of salvation by trusting and accepting Christ.

3. Dwells in All Believers Forever

The indwelling Spirit is a gift (not merit earned) from God to all believers, not just a select few (**John 7:37–39: Acts 11:17; Romans 5:5; I Corinthians 2:12; 2 Corinthians 5:5**) "*Do you not know that you are God's temple and that God's Spirit dwells in you?*" (**1 Corinthians 3:16**)

This indwelling is forever. **John 14:16** provides that awesome truth from Jesus the night before He was crucified, *"And I will ask the Father, and He will give you another Comforter, that He may be with you forever."* This reality ought to give believers (a) a sense of eternal security in their relationship with God, (b) a motivation to practice this close presence of God, and (c) a sensitivity to sins against God.

4.   **Fills Believers**

Ephesians 5:18 informs us, *"And do not get drunk with wine, for that is debauchery, but be filled with the Spirit."* Being filled with the Spirit does not mean you have more or less of the Spirit, who is a person who cannot be divided into parts. It means that you yield/surrender to the control of the Spirit in varying degrees.

It is like putting an Alka Seltzer in water. It permeates the water, and the water takes on the characteristics of the Alka Seltzer. Or like a glove playing the piano which is impossible until a skillful hand fills the glove.

Being drunk with wine controls our thoughts and actions, which brings out our fleshly weakness, but God's desire is that we be filled with the Spirit and let Him control our thoughts and actions, which brings out His power.

It is obvious that all believers do not have the same degree of spirituality, wisdom, or surrender to the Lord. The difference is related to the work of the Holy Spirit in a person's heart. Every Christian is indwelt with the Holy Spirit, but every Christian does not heed the direction and instruction of the Holy Spirit. Accordingly, those who listen to the world rather than to the Holy

Spirit are worldly or fleshly, and those yielded to the control of the Holy Spirit can be spiritually minded and "*Walk in the Spirit*" (**Galatians 5:16**).

The apostle Peter presents a good model. Peter constantly wanted to be where Jesus was. Why? Because he had no power without Jesus.

a) Peter did miracles with Jesus — Walked on water (**Matthew 14:29**).

b) Peter said miraculous truths with Jesus — "*Thou art the Christ, the Son of the living God*" (**Matthew 16:16–17**).

c) Peter had miraculous courage with Jesus — He tried to fight soldiers of the Roman army in the Garden of Gethsemane (**John 18:10**).

What happened when Peter was not with Jesus? He, by himself, was so weak that he even denied knowing Jesus (**Mark 14:66–72**). He had no power. But observe what happened beginning in **Acts** after Jesus had ascended from the earth.

a) Peter did miraculous things. He healed. (**Acts 3:1–11**).

b) Peter said miraculous things. He preached and 3,000 were saved (**Acts 2:14–47**).

c) Peter has miraculous courage. He preached of Jesus before the Sanhedrin (**Acts 4:5–21**).

What caused Peter to perform as he did in Jesus' presence? He had been filled with the Holy Spirit (**Acts 2:4**). He discovered the secret of the Spirit-filled life—Jesus' consciousness, saturation with the presence and Word of Jesus Christ.

As Jesus instructs in **John 15:5**, *".... apart from me (Jesus) you can do nothing."* It is basically a lifestyle of "Let go, let God." This is trusting your life to God. Being filled with the Spirit practically is a daily surrender to God which aligns us to seek the eternal and not the temporal of this broken world. It is an ongoing, moment-by-moment process of continually trusting God with our lives and choices and keeping our focus on the eternal. **In essence, being filled with the Spirit is not that we get more of God, but God gets more of us.**

5.   Teaches and Reminds

In **John 14:26**, Jesus told his disciples, *"But the Helper, the Holy Spirit, whom the Father will send in my name, He will teach you all things and bring to your remembrance all that I have said to you."*

The Greek word "Parakletos" in this passage is translated as "Helper" in the English Standard Version, "Advocate" in the New International Version, and "Counselor" in the King James Version. The meaning of this word relates to "legal counsel." The Holy Spirit provides wise counsel to Christ's followers. Jesus knew He would be going away and that His followers would need the Holy Spirit as a helper and an advocate to remind them of His teachings. What better teacher can you have than the person who inspired (God-breathed) all the books of the Bible? *"All scripture is inspired by God and profitable for teaching, for reproof, for correction, for training in righteousness"* **(2 Timothy 3:16).** *"For no prophecy was ever made by an act of human will, but men moved by the Holy Spirit spoke from God"* **(2 Peter 1:21).** *"When we tell you these things, not in words taught by human wisdom. Instead, we speak words given us by the Holy Spirit, using the Spirit's words to explain spiritual truths"* **(1 Corinthians 2:13).**

6. Source of Power, Wisdom, and Revelation.

"These are the things God has revealed to us by His Spirit. The Spirit searches all things, even the deep things of God. For who knows a person's thoughts except for their own spirit within them? In the same way, no one knows the thoughts of God except the Spirit of God" (**1 Corinthians 2:10–11**).

God gives His followers the Holy Spirit, so we may know Him better. Since the Holy Spirit is God's Spirit, He knows the thoughts of God and reveals those thoughts to believers. The Holy Spirit opens believers' eyes to the hope of salvation and their inheritance in Christ.

Christians have access to power, wisdom, and revelation from the Holy Spirit, just as the Apostle Paul wrote to believers in Ephesus, *"I keep asking that the God of our Lord Jesus Christ, the glorious Father, may give you the Spirit of wisdom and revelation, so that you may know Him better. I pray that the eyes of your heart may be enlightened in order that you may know the hope to which He has called you, the riches of His glorious inheritance in His holy people, and His incomparably great power for us who believe. That power is the same as the mighty strength He exerted when He raised Christ from the dead and seated Him at his right hand in the heavenly realms"* (**Ephesians 1:17–20**).

The Greek word "dunamis" is the English word "power" in "His incomparably great power" in this scripture. "Dunamis" is also used for dynamite. In essence, we have the dynamite of God available through the Holy Spirit, who indwells us.

We all have lights, air conditioning, and electrical appliances that we use regularly in our normal daily lives. When the electrical power source goes off for whatever reason, it disrupts our temporal lives immensely. When we are not plugged into the power source of God, His Holy Spirit, it disrupts our spiritual lives immensely. **We plug into God's power source through FAITH which is believing and trusting God to be involved in every temporal or spiritual step we take in our life journey.**

"Faith sees the invisible, believes the incredible, and receives the impossible." --- **Corrie Ten Boom,** Dutch resistance hero and Christian writer

7. Guides to All Truth and Knowledge.

The Holy Spirit is called the *"Spirit of Truth"* in **John 16:13** because He guides believers into all truth. Jesus told his disciples the Holy Spirit would make known what He hears and would only speak what the Father speaks. *"But when He, the Spirit of truth, comes, He will guide you into all the truth. He will not speak on His own; He will speak only what He hears, and He will tell you what is yet to come. He will glorify Me because it is from Me that He will receive what He will make known to you. All that belongs to the Father is Mine. That is why I said the Spirit will receive from Me what He will make known to you"* (**John 16:13–15**).

8. Gives Spiritual Gifts to Believers.

Someone once said that American football is a game in which 50,000 people desperately needing exercise sit in the bleachers and watch 22 men who are desperately needing rest. The same can be said for the church. The masses sit in the pews rooting for a struggling few who are upfront trying to do God's work. Obviously, this is not God's plan. Instead, He has provided a way for every single Christian to be equipped to be a part of the "game" to have a role in serving Him. The means is the spiritual gift (or gifts) that every Christian is given when he/she accepts Jesus Christ as his/her Savior.

The Holy Spirit **sovereignly chooses (1 Corinthians 12:11) and gifts** His attributes and characteristics in the lives of every believer (**1 Corinthians 12:7**). Nothing is left to mere human choice or judgment. The composite of these gifts in the church/body of Christ (**1 Corinthians 12:27**) manifests the total person of Jesus. A gift is a supernatural ability to serve the Lord by being His physical representative in serving others whereby God may be glorified through Jesus Christ (**1 Peter 4:11**). It is not for our personal glory. Your spiritual gift (or gifts) is not what God expects from you; it is what God wants to do through you. The gifts of the Spirit must always be exercised in love (**1 Corinthians 13**).

Bible Verses about the Gifts of the Holy Spirit

- *"To one there is given through the Spirit a message of wisdom, to another a message of knowledge by means of the same Spirit, to another faith by the same Spirit, to another gifts of healing by that one Spirit, to another miraculous powers, to another prophecy, to another distinguishing between spirits, to another speaking in different kinds of tongues, and to still another the interpretation of tongues"* (**1 Corinthians 12:8–10**).

- *"The Spirit of the LORD will rest on him — the Spirit of wisdom and of understanding, the Spirit of counsel and of might, the Spirit of the knowledge and fear of the LORD — and he will delight in the fear of the LORD. He will not judge by what he sees with his eyes or decide by what he hears with his ears"* (**Isaiah 11:2–3**).

- *"But to each one of us grace has been given as Christ apportioned it. This is why it says: 'When He ascended on high, He took many captives and gave gifts to His people.' What does "He ascended" mean except that He also descended to the lower, earthly regions? He who descended is the very one who ascended higher than all the heavens, to fill the whole universe. Christ Himself gave the apostles, the prophets, the evangelists, the pastors and teachers, to equip His people for works of service, so that the body of Christ may be built up until we all reach unity in the faith and in the knowledge of the Son of God and become mature, attaining to the whole measure of the fullness of Christ"* **(Ephesians 4:7–13).**

- *"For by the grace given me I say to every one of you: Do not think of yourself more highly than you ought, but rather think of yourself with sober judgment, in accordance with the faith God has distributed to each of you. For just as each of us has one body with many members, and these members do not all have the same function, so in Christ we, though many, form one body, and each member belongs to all the others. We have different gifts, according to the grace given to each of us. If your gift is prophesying, then prophesy in accordance with your faith; if it is serving, then serve; if it is teaching, then teach; if it is to encourage, then give encouragement; if it is giving, then give generously; if it is to lead, do it diligently; if it is to show mercy, do it cheerfully"* **(Romans 12:3–8).**

These spiritual gifts listed in the preceding Bible verses demonstrate significant overlap as well as important variations. This suggests that none of the lists, taken either individually or together, is intended to be comprehensive. Rather each is indicative of the diversity of ways God endows Christians with spiritual service.

The Gifts of the Holy Spirit

There is some dispute as to the exact nature and number of gifts of the Holy Spirit, but here is a list of spiritual gifts referenced in the preceding Bible verses and their essential meanings.

The Gift of Wisdom — the divine ability to see things from God's perspective and make choices and give leadership that is according to God's perspective.

The Gift of Knowledge — the divine ability to comprehensively understand a spiritual issue or circumstance, not dependent on I.Q.

The Gift of Faith — the divine ability to trust God and inspire others to trust God, no matter the conditions, fully expecting God to handle the obstacles. Every believer should walk by faith, and each has a measure of faith, but not all have the gift of faith.

The Gift of Healing — the divine ability to use God's healing power to cure a person who is ill, wounded, or suffering. A believer today cannot necessarily expect to be healed. If it were God's will to heal every believer, then no believer would ever die. To disregard human means for healing and simply pray for a miraculous cure is like praying for a harvest and then sitting in a rocking chair, refusing to plant or cultivate the ground. We need to pray for God's best in our healing prayers.

The Gift of Miracles — the divine ability to display signs and miracles that give credibility to God's Word and the Gospel message, primarily for the benefit of unbelievers. Praying in faith with power, especially for God's supernatural intervention in impossible situations.

The Gift of Prophecy — the divine ability to declare or proclaim revealed words from God that convince unbelievers while challenging and comforting believers, giving forth God's message—preaching. Different from being a prophet who foretells future truths.

The Gift of Discernment — the divine ability to recognize whether something is truly from God and in accordance with righteousness, distinguishing right from wrong based on God's Word.

The Gift of Tongues — the divine ability to communicate in a foreign language you do not have experience with, to converse with those who speak that language.

The Gift of Interpreting Tongues — the divine ability to interpret the speech and writings of a different language and translate it back to others in your own language.

The Gift of Administration – the divine ability to understand the details of what makes a church function — planning and executing procedures that increase organizational effectiveness.

The Gift of Hospitality — the divine ability to make others feel warmly welcomed, accepted, and comfortable in the church family—coordinating factors that promote fellowship, food, or shelter.

The Gift of Helps/Serving — the divine ability to recognize needs with the desire and capacity to always help others and do whatever it takes to achieve a task without the need for recognition.

The Gift of Teaching — the divine ability to educate God's people by clearly explaining and applying the Bible in a way that helps them to learn.

The Gift of Pastoring — the divine ability to be a shepherd and care for the spiritual well-being of a body of God's people (their flock) and to equip them for ministry.

The Gift of Exhortation/Encouragement — the divine ability to motivate God's people who are discouraged or wavering in their journey with God. The ability to bring out the best in others and challenge them to develop their potential.

The Gift of Giving — the divine ability that has "unusual" generosity (beyond tithing) at its center focused on the temporal and eternal needs of others. All Christians should imitate Christ in sacrificial giving, even without the spiritual gift. Giving should be with a cheerful heart with no thought of return or self-gain.

The Gift of Leadership — the divine ability to clarify and communicate the vision of a ministry in a way that attracts and motivates others to get involved.

The Gift of Evangelism — the divine ability that empowers the person to always, with exceptional clarity, be telling others about the "good news" of salvation through Christ. Whether or not one has this gift, all believers are commanded by Jesus to be witnesses.

The Gift of Mercy — the divine ability to detect hurt, empathize with those who are suffering, and provide compassionate and cheerful support to those in distress, crisis, or pain.

The Gift of Distinguishing Between Spirits — the divine ability to tell the difference between doctrine from the Holy Spirit and false doctrine from men and/or Satan.

The Gift of Being an Apostle — the divine ability provided to the original custodians of the authentic gospel, witnesses of Jesus' resurrection. If this ability is gifted today, it would be the divine ability to start churches and missions in a variety of different cultures.

How do you identify your spiritual gift(s)? God wants you to use your gifts; He doesn't hide them. I have done a few assessments, and if this is something you feel inclined to do, search for "spiritual gifts tests and assessments" in your computer search engine, and you will find innumerable free ones to help you. However, **God is the one that reveals our gifts through opportunities and instills passion in us around the gifts that He has given us**.

Not knowing our gifts is not the problem; not using our gifts in the opportunities that God provides is the problem. In my personal experience and observation, you must be actively involved in the Word of God. You are seeking to glorify God. You are associating with believers. You are presenting yourself as available for service in the group. You regularly confess your sins so that these do not become a roadblock to exercising your gifts. You have a spiritual passion in particular areas. Then your question is changed to "What in this situation that God has placed me are the opportunities for serving others in word and deed?" God truly does want to use us in the spiritual gift(s) He has given us and developed a passion in us for it or them. **God does not hide these gifts from us; He provides opportunities to exercise them.**

"Your spiritual gifts were not given for your own benefit but for the benefit of others, just as other people were given gifts for your benefit." — **Rick Warren,** American pastor and writer

Even individually, not having all these spiritual gifts doesn't give us an excuse not to display the characteristics of Christ. As we grow spiritually, we begin to look more and more like Christ in many of these areas of spiritual gifting.

9. Grows the Fruit of the Spirit in Believers

"Fruit is always the miraculous, the created; it is never the result of willing, but always a growth. The fruit of the Spirit is a gift of God, and only He can produce it. They who bear it know as little about it as the tree knows of its fruit. They know only the power of Him on whom their life depends." — **Dietrich Bonhoeffer,** German theologian

Unlike the gifts of the Spirit, the fruit of the Spirit is not divided among believers. Instead, all Christians should be marked by all the fruit of the Spirit. **The fruit of the Spirit is God's expectations in our lives.**

The Holy Spirit works in our lives to produce the fruit of the Spirit. There are two passages of Scripture that are especially helpful to see this.

Psalm 1:2–3 compares the Godly man to a tree planted by a river: *"But his delight is in the Law of the Lord, and on His Law he meditates* (not just reads*) day and night. He will be like a tree planted by streams of water, which yields its fruit in its season, and its leaf does not wither; and in whatever he does, he prospers."* **Apart from the Word of God, there will be no lasting spiritual growth or fruit-bearing in our lives.**

John 15:4–5 compares our relationship to Him to the branches of a vine. *"Get your life from Me (Abide in Me) and I will live in you. No branch can give fruit by itself. It has to get life from the vine. You are able to give fruit only when you have life from Me. I am the Vine and you are the branches. Get your life from Me. Then I will live in you, and you will give much fruit. You can do nothing without Me."*

As we, through obedient living, abide in Christ (like life-giving sap in a vine), the Spirit flows into us, producing fruit to the glory of the Father and the nourishment and blessing of others.

Of all the passages in the Bible which sketch the character of Christ and the fruit which the Spirit brings to our lives, none is more compact and challenging than **Galatians 5:22–23,** "But the fruit of the Spirit is love, joy, peace, forbearance, kindness, goodness, faithfulness, gentleness, and self-control. Against such things there is no law."

The Fruit of the Spirit

Love

Love is the love of God and of neighbor, without any thought of receiving something in return. It is not a "warm and fuzzy" emotional feeling; love is expressed in concrete action toward God and our fellow man.

"Love is patient, love is kind. It does not envy, it does not boast, it is not proud. It does not dishonor others, it is not self-seeking, it is not easily angered, it keeps no record of wrongs. Love does not delight in evil but rejoices with the truth. It always protects, always trusts, always hopes, always perseveres" (**1 Corinthians 13:4–7**).

"And above all things have fervent love for one another, for 'love will cover a multitude of sins'" (**1 Peter 4:8**).

"If we don't have the Word of God as the foundation of what we believe, we will have a faulty footing—it will not stand against the elements that will come against us. God has designed both our physical and spiritual lives to be ordered by one key attribute upon which the fruit of the Spirit is based — that foundation is love." — **David Jeremiah,** pastor and television/radio broadcaster

Joy

Joy isn't emotional in the sense that we commonly think of joy. Rather, it is the state of being undisturbed by the negative things in life. **It is the inner stability of knowing that God is in control and sovereign.**

JOY is a good acronym for **J**esus **O**wns **Y**ou, and therefore, your life priorities are **J**esus **O**thers **Y**ourself in descending order.

"Now may the God of hope fill you with all joy and peace in believing, so that you will abound in hope by the power of the Holy Spirit" (**Romans 15:13**).

"Count it all joy when you fall into various trials" (**James 1:2**).

Peace

Peace is tranquility in our soul that comes from relying on God. Rather than getting caught up in anxiety for the future, Christians, through the prompting of the Holy Spirit, trust God to provide for them.

"You will keep him in perfect peace, whose mind is stayed on You, because he trusts in You" (**Isaiah 26:3**).

"Be anxious for nothing, but in everything by prayer and supplication with thanksgiving let your requests be made known to God. And the peace of God, which surpasses all comprehension, will guard your hearts and your minds in Christ Jesus" (**Philippians 4:6–7**).

"Let the peace of Christ rule in your hearts, to which indeed you were called in one body; and be thankful" (**Colossians 3:15**).

Patience

Patience is the ability to wait on God in His perfect timing. It also involves bearing the imperfections of other people through a knowledge of our own imperfections and our need for God's mercy and forgiveness.

"Rest in the LORD and wait patiently for Him; do not fret because of him who prospers in his way, because of the man who carries out wicked schemes" (**Psalm 37:7**).

"Here is the patience of the saints; here are those who keep the commandments of God and the faith of Jesus" (**Revelation 14:12**).

"The Lord is not slow about His promise, as some count slowness, but is patient toward you, not wishing for any to perish but for all to come to repentance" (**2 Peter 3:9**).

Kindness

Kindness is compassion in the involvement with others. It is love enduring which washes away all that is harsh and austere.

"Be kind to one another, tender-hearted, forgiving each other, just as God in Christ also has forgiven you" (**Ephesians 4:32**).

"Those who are kind benefit themselves, but the cruel bring ruin on themselves" (**Proverbs 11:17**).

"Love is patient, love is kind…" (**1 Corinthians 13:4**).

Goodness

Goodness is that quality that always strives for the highest moral and ethical values. Goodness, unlike kindness, sometimes involves harshness (in love). *"Surely goodness and loving kindness will follow me all the days of my life, and I will dwell in the house of the LORD forever"* (**Psalm 23:6**).

"Who among you is wise and understanding? Let him show by his good behavior his deeds in the gentleness of wisdom" (**James 3:13**).

"Do not remember the sins of my youth or my transgressions; according to Your lovingkindness remember me, for Your goodness' sake, O LORD" (**Psalm 25:7**).

Faithfulness

Faithfulness, as a fruit of the Holy Spirit, means living our life in accordance with God's will at all times. Lack of faithfulness is a sign of spiritual immaturity.

"A faithful man will abound with blessings, but he who makes haste to be rich will not go unpunished" (**Proverbs 28:20**).

"For we walk by faith, not by sight" (**2 Corinthians 5:7**).

"Most men will proclaim each his own goodness, but who can find a faithful man?" (**Proverbs 20:6**).

Gentleness

Gentleness is being mild in behavior and forgiving rather than angry, gracious rather than vengeful. The gentle person is meek; like Christ, he does not insist on having his own way but yields to others for the sake of the Kingdom of God. Meekness is strength under control.

"Let your gentleness be evident to all. The Lord is near" (**Philippians 4:5**).

"...to be peaceable, gentle, showing every consideration for all men" (**Titus 3:2**).

"A gentle answer turns away wrath, but a harsh word stirs up anger" (**Proverbs 15:1**).

Self-control

Self-control means having mastery and being able to control one's thoughts and actions.

"Like a city that is broken into and without walls is a man who has no control over his spirit" (**Proverbs 25:28**).

"He who is slow to anger is better than the mighty, and he who rules his spirit, than he who captures a city" (**Proverbs 16:32**).

When God indwells us, and we spend more and more time with Him, we begin to live out His attributes (Fruit of the Spirit). A lack of fruit in a Christian's life shows a waning (or even lack) of a relationship with the indwelling Holy Spirit.

10. Seals Ownership of Believers to God

In ancient times, a seal was a "legal signature" attesting ownership and validating what was sealed. The Holy Spirit is our mark of adoption as God's children. Jesus sent the Holy Spirit to his followers so that they could be confident in their salvation. Just as you might make a deposit or a down payment on a new car to make sure the salesperson doesn't sell it to anyone else, the Holy Spirit is a deposit in our lives confirming the validity of Christ's message and that we belong to Christ. *"And you also were included in Christ when you heard the message of truth, the gospel of your salvation. When you believed, you were marked in him with a seal, the promised Holy Spirit, who is a deposit guaranteeing our inheritance until the redemption of those who are God's possession—to the praise of his glory"* (**Ephesians 1:13**).

"Don't let obstacles along the road to eternity shake your confidence in God's promise. The Holy Spirit is God's seal that you will arrive." — **David Jeremiah,** American Christian author and pastor

11.   Helps with Our Weaknesses and Intercedes for Us

We all have times when we feel weak and don't know what to do. The Holy Spirit helps us align with God's will by interceding for us during those times. *"In the same way, the Spirit helps us in our weakness. We do not know what we ought to pray for, but the Spirit Himself intercedes for us through wordless groans. And He who searches our hearts knows the mind of the Spirit because the Spirit intercedes for God's people in accordance with the will of God"* **(Romans 8:26–27)**.

12.   Sanctifies Believers and Grants Us Eternal Life

The Holy Spirit works in the lives of believers to renew, sanctify, and make us holy. Just as the Holy Spirit raised Christ from the dead, the Holy Spirit will give eternal life to believers in Christ. *"But if Christ is in you, then even though your body is subject to death because of sin, the Spirit gives life because of righteousness. And if the Spirit of Him who raised Jesus from the dead is living in you, He who raised Christ from the dead will also give life to your mortal bodies because of His Spirit who lives in you"* **(Romans 8:10–11)**.

Sanctification by the Holy Spirit is the second part of the salvation process, which saves us from the power of sin; after justification which saves us from the penalty of sin; and finally, the third part of glorification when we go to Heaven, which saves us from the presence of sin.

13.   Provides Power to be Witnesses for Christ

Jesus knew that His disciples, throughout time, would need God's power to carry out their mission to be witnesses to the entire world. Jesus told his disciples, *"But you will receive power when the Holy Spirit comes on you, and you will be my witnesses in Jerusalem, and in all Judea and Samaria, and to the ends of the earth"* (**Acts 1:8**).

SPIRITUAL BREATHING

Because God loves us, He doesn't want to have our fellowship and communication with Him severed. The key for many in experiencing God's presence and direction moment by moment is something called "**spiritual breathing,**" which is a phrase coined by **Bill Bright**, the founder of CRU (Campus Crusade for Christ).

Regular breathing has two parts: exhaling impure air and inhaling pure air. Spiritually, we become aware of an impure attitude or area of our life that displeases the Lord, so we need to "exhale" or, in other words, confess that sin to God. Confession means to agree with God that we have sinned and admit we now want to change: *"If we confess our sin to God, He is faithful and righteous to forgive us our sins and to cleanse us from all unrighteousness"* (**1 John 1:9**).

The second part of spiritual breathing is, obviously, to "inhale." This refers to a prayer of willing surrender to God's control. Through prayer, we can ask the Holy Spirit to run our lives and take over. The key to the process of spiritual breathing lies in surrendering that control to God on a consistent and regular basis.

Spiritually, we must surrender and yield our lives to the control of the Spirit. We must let the searchlight of God's Word scan us to detect the abiding sins and fruitless qualities which impair our personal growth and fruitfulness. Not until we have allowed our old selves to be crucified with Christ can our new selves emerge to display the marvelous fruit characteristics of Jesus Christ. And only the Holy Spirit can make possible the living out of Christ's love; this can never be produced by human effort.

In summary, every believer in Christ has the ever-present travel companion, the Holy Spirit, eternally working in his/her surrendered life to provide His presence, His power, His gifting, and His fruit to allow us to journey in abundant life for the glory of the triune God.

SOME PERSONAL STEPS IN SHOE LEATHER

My belief in the intimacy and power of God was brought to full reality when I became aware (many years after I had accepted Christ as my savior) that He had indwelled me permanently with His Holy Spirit.

I had not realized that I had access to the power of God living in me until I got deeply involved in God's Word, which grew my faith (believing and trusting God). Since coming to that exciting revelation, I am seeing the power of God working through me, a very ordinary person, to do extraordinary things when I plug into His power source through faith. God has allowed me opportunities around the world to tell of some of my personal journeys, especially in business. The Holy Spirit always uses these times for His multiplication purposes. In essence, He allows me to toss a tiny pebble into the water, and He causes the ripple effect for His glory.

He has sovereignly chosen to give me spiritual gifts that include teaching, encouragement, faith, and giving so that I can serve the Lord in His power for His glory.

Our Heavenly Father loves to use all His children in supernatural eternal ways for His glory.

CHAPTER 6.

TALKING ALONG THE WAY

"Prayer is simply talking to God like a friend and should be the easiest thing we do each day." — **Joyce Meyer,** American author

Jesus' closest relationships on earth were built as He walked with people day after day, developing deep friendships, talking as they journeyed, and doing things side-by-side. God the Holy Spirit, who indwells us forever after salvation through Christ, is now our traveling companion with whom we can converse, and He helps us when we struggle with what to say in our talking with the triune God through prayer (**Romans 8:26**). The operation of the Spirit is the key to prayer. That's because a spiritual prayer cannot be offered unless it is motivated by this Spirit—the Holy Spirit of God.

Of course, anyone of all religions and beliefs, even atheists, can offer prayers to God. In a manner of speaking, we can say that God is capable of hearing all people's prayers simply because he is God. Jesus tells us that God gives the rain and sunshine to all, even the unrighteous (**Matthew 5:45**).

But while anyone can pray to God, a righteous person—made so by new birth and the indwelling of the Holy Spirit—has a special blessing in prayer.

"The prayer of a righteous man is powerful and effective" (**James 5:16**). In fact, the prayer that fully communicates with God must be offered in the Spirit.

If we have the Holy Spirit working in our minds and hearts, we talk with God as our Heavenly Father. Paul says, "*God sent the Spirit of his Son into our hearts, the Spirit who calls out, 'Abba, Father'*" (**Galatians 4:6**). This Spirit "*testifies with our spirit that we are God's children*" (**Romans 8:16**). Prayer, then, has a special meaning if we are God's spiritual children. We can talk with God as a child does with his or her father.

Saying that you can experience being a child of God without learning to pray is like saying you can be happily married or have a deep friendship without regular communication. Learning how to pray is about developing a relationship with God. Relationships are built on moments of connection. Those moments of connection bond you to another person, and many of them center on communication—the words you say and the way you say them.

Prayer is our direct line with heaven. Prayer is a communication process that allows us to talk to our Heavenly Father. He wants us to communicate with Him, like a person-to-person phone call. Cell phones and other devices have become a necessity for people today. We have Bluetooth devices, iPhones, and talking computers. These are means of communication that allow two or more people to interact, discuss, and respond to one another. To pray is simply to communicate with God.

Newsweek magazine reported, "More Americans will pray than will go to work, or exercise, or have sexual relations." So many Americans (78 percent) say they pray that prayer has become a news item. ***Newsweek*** even devoted a cover story to the subject: "Talking to God: An Intimate Look at the Way We Pray." They figured that people would want to read about prayer. And the word "*with*" is the operative one here. To make an important point, prayer is talking "*with*" God and not just "*to*" God, as the *Newsweek* title had it.

More than this, Christian prayer is talking with the God of the Bible. It is a conversation with the supreme Creator of the universe, and the Father of Jesus Christ, who is also God (**John 1:1**). That such contact is possible between us humans and this awesome God is a wonderful mystery. We, who are spiritually flawed, have access to this all-mighty God and can come into His holy presence. The New Testament tells us we can enter God's presence because Jesus paid for our sins and reconciled us to God by His death on the cross (**Hebrews 10:19–22**). Through Christ, said the apostle Paul, we have "access to the Father by one Spirit" (**Ephesians 2:18**).

Prayer is a supernatural activity where you are talking with the God of the universe, who is unlike anyone else with whom you could ever talk. He has a personality and qualities with which you can understand and relate. But you cannot expect to relate to God in exactly the way you might to a close friend or family member. He's so much bigger and more incredible than that. He is beyond what you can understand in the natural everyday world. He is supernatural.

Even if talking with other people comes very naturally to you, it's understandable if talking with God feels difficult. He is not visible to our human eyes. And He speaks to us differently than other people. Remember that our Heavenly Father loves us more than we love ourselves and wants us to tell Him about everything. He is an excellent listener.

"If we knew how much God loved us and was for us, we'd talk to Him all day long." —**Donald Miller,** American writer

Prayer isn't a ritual that depends on closing our eyes and putting on holy faces. We don't have to kneel or sit. We can pray while walking, driving, or working. God responds to a two-word cry for help in the middle of a busy afternoon, just like He does to a focused prayer time after reading Scripture in the morning. Praying doesn't have to be complicated. God delights in any simple words we offer Him.

Communicating with God can mean thanking Him, praising Him, confessing something you've done wrong, or expressing a need you have. It can even mean just talking to Him as you would to a friend.

"Prayer is intimacy with God." — **Jim Maxim**, Acts413 Ministries

Whatever is on your mind matters to God because you matter to Him. As you develop the habit of praying, over time, you will gain a sense of what things God is talking to you about and what He thinks is worth your attention. In the beginning, try not to get too hung up on what you should be praying about. God has all the time in the world, and He's far more patient with us than we are with ourselves.

But if you're ever in doubt about what to pray, pray like Jesus.

Jesus' closest friends, the men he focused most of his attention on, faced the same problem we do. So, they asked Jesus to teach them how to pray. The result is the best-known prayer in human history — what we call the **Lord's Prayer**.

"This, then, is how you should pray: "Our Father in heaven, hallowed be your name, your kingdom come, your will be done, on earth as it is in heaven. Give us today our daily bread. And forgive us our debts, as we also have forgiven our debtors. And lead us not into temptation but deliver us from the evil one" (**Matthew 6:9–13**).

Looking at Jesus' prayer piece by piece provides some shoe leather for the prayer lives of His followers then and now.

Here are eight lessons on prayer that we can learn from the example Jesus gives us in **Matthew 6:9–13**:

1. *Our Father in Heaven*

Jesus starts by establishing our identity as children of God. He is stressing the importance of really owning this belief as a source of confidence that when you pray, your Father in Heaven will listen.

2. *Hallowed be Your Name*

Hallowed means holy or sanctified. God's name is holy, as God is the epitome of sanctity. *"There is no one holy like the Lord"* (**1 Samuel 2:2**). We, as Christians, understand that the Almighty Father is to be revered and praised above all else. In this petition, we pray that the entire world will recognize the holy name of God as the one true God of all, the Creator and Ruler of the universe.

3. *Your Kingdom Come*

This petition is two-fold. First, we pray for the Kingdom of God to take form in the here and now so that we can live in a world characterized by faith, hope, and love. (**1 Corinthians 13:13**).

Second, we pray that the promise of a "new heaven and a new earth" be fulfilled. When that promise is fulfilled, the faithful will live with God in His Kingdom eternally as members of a Holy City in which there is no death, crying, or pain. (**Revelation 21:1–4**).

4.   *Your Will Be Done on Earth as it Is in Heaven*

God reigns from Heaven with compassion and justice (**Isaiah 30:18**). His will is that we praise Him and love one another. We know this because Jesus summarized the entirety of God's Word into two commands — *love God with all your heart, soul, and mind, and love your neighbor as yourself* (**Matthew 22:37–40**).

Praying this petition is an act of selfless surrender to the will of God. We humbly request here for God to give us the strength to follow His will, not ours, in living a life that glorifies Him and shows compassion and justice to others. In addition, we are pleading with our Sovereign God to bring the sinlessness and love of Heaven to Earth.

5.   *Give Us Today Our Daily Bread*

Just as good food nourishes the body, the "Good News" nourishes the soul. The Bible instructs that "*man shall not live on bread alone but on every word that comes from the mouth of God*" (**Deuteronomy 8:3**).

In this appeal, we pray for spiritual sustenance so that we can have the fortitude to go out into the world and spread His Message through our words and actions. This nourishment comes from the Word of God and from communion with Christ, who is the "bread of life" that comes down from Heaven so that "*whoever feeds on this bread will live forever*" (**John 6:48–58**).

Also, in this appeal, He encourages us to pray for our temporal needs (not wants) focused on our daily dependence on God.

6.   *And Forgive Us Our Debts, As We Also Have Forgiven Our Debtors*

This section of the Lord's Prayer may be the toughest to pray and follow. However, this request contains much wisdom. The debt doesn't necessarily involve money; it could be something someone literally took from you. More often, it will be some way in which you feel someone has hurt you.

While anyone can ask to receive forgiveness, reflecting on the way we forgive others can lead us to patience and grace, which can be transformative. Forgiveness was at the heart of Jesus' teaching during His time on earth, and so we find it here at the heart of His guide to prayer. For times when forgiving someone proves especially difficult, the Bible teaches that a good time to extend forgiveness is during prayer when our minds and hearts are united with God **(Mark 11:25)**.

By choosing to replace resentment and bitterness with forgiveness, we reflect God's love and mercy in our actions. This, in turn, enables us to walk more confidently toward God, who wants our every step to be toward Him.

7.   *And Lead Us Not into Temptation*

Temptation can cause us to sin and lead us away from God in ways that can be cumulative. God doesn't lead us to sin; we do that all on our own because of the freedom of choice our Creator gave us.

But our God is faithful and promises to provide a way out of any temptation that we may face **(1 Corinthians 10:13)**. In this supplication, we acknowledge that our freedom of choice brings with it human weaknesses. To overcome those weaknesses, we pray here for God to extend His guiding hand over us and grant us the discernment necessary to steer clear of temptation and sin.

8.   *But Deliver Us from the Evil One*

We are in a spiritual battle, and we have a very real enemy from whom we need God's deliverance. This petition covers the many times that we do fall prey to temptation and sin. During these times of entanglement, if we continually seek the Lord, He will answer us and deliver us from all of our fears (**Psalm 34:4**).

In this appeal, we ask, during those times when we're mired in sin, that the Almighty Father will reach down and liberate us from evil's grip. This petition is also one for protection, as we ask God to protect us from the devil's grasp in all future circumstances.

The Lord's Prayer Meaning.

The Lord's Prayer is much more than a handy guide on what to pray when no other words come to mind.

The prayer, if we meditate on each petition, serves as a moral compass that reveals the best way to go before the Father in requesting His guidance and protection.

The Lord's Prayer focuses our thoughts on what's important in life by summarizing all that we must do to be "good and faithful servants," namely: revere God, accept His will, know His Word, love each other through forgiveness, and resist evil.

LISTENING TO GOD

Prayer is communication with God; it not only involves talking with God but also listening to God.

According to Jesus, we are His sheep, the flock of His pasture. **John 10** expands on this wonderful theme. As Jesus's sheep, we should be able to listen to His voice and follow Him because we clearly recognize his voice. *"The gatekeeper opens the gate for Jesus, and the sheep listen to His voice. He calls His own sheep by name and leads them out. When He has brought out all his own, He goes on ahead of them, and His sheep follow Him because they know His voice"* **(John 10:3–4).**

In the next verse, Jesus makes the point that we should not follow any other voice. *"But they will never follow a stranger; in fact, they will run away from him because they do not recognize a stranger's voice"* **(John 10:5).**

Later, Jesus alludes to the Gentiles, who will also hear His voice and follow Him. *"I have other sheep that are not of this sheep pen. I must bring them also. They too will listen to My voice, and there shall be one flock and One Shepherd"* **(John 10:16).**

Our Lord Jesus is very happy to lead us as His disciples. We who follow Him should be able to hear His voice and receive the guidance we need. It is part of our birthright when we are born again by the Holy Spirit and become followers of Jesus. But what about those other voices? How can we be sure we are hearing only from our Lord?

The best way to listen to God's voice is through the Bible, but God can speak to you in different ways. Rarely can we expect an audible voice, but He may talk to you through thoughts in your mind, through other people (even if they don't realize it), through books, music, sermons, circumstances, etc.

The Bible is the Word of God, His revelation to us, breathed out by His Holy Spirit through human authors (**2 Timothy 3:16–17**). The first step you need to take is to learn how to identify the true voice of God as He communicated through Scripture. To be able to identify the true voice of God, you need to read the Bible. Then, if what you've heard goes against what the Bible teaches, you will know that it wasn't the voice of the Lord (**John 10:4–5,7–8,14**).

We need to take time to be quiet after reading the Bible to hear from God. God cannot be heard in noise and restlessness. He will speak to us if we give Him a chance, if we will listen, and if we will be quiet.

"*Be still*," the psalmist wrote, "*and know that I am God*" (**Psalm 46:10**). "*Listen, listen to me*," God pleads, "*and eat what is good, and your soul will delight in the richest of fare. Give ear and come to me; hear me, that your soul may live*" (**Isaiah 55:2–3**).

Listen to Him. "*When your words came, I ate them*," said Jeremiah (**Jeremiah 15:16**). The problem with many of us is that though we read God's Word, we're not feeding on the words of God.

The main purpose of reading and studying the Bible, however, is not to accumulate data about Him but to "come to Him" to encounter Him as our living God.

Jesus said to some Bible students of His day, *"You diligently study the Scriptures because you think that by them you possess eternal life. These are the Scriptures that testify about me"* (**John 5:39**).

The scholars read the Bible, but they didn't listen to God; they *"never heard his voice"* (**John 5:37**). We should do more than read words; we should seek the Word exposed in the words. We want to move beyond information to seeing God and being informed and shaped by His truth.

There's a passing exhilaration — the "joy of discovery" — in acquiring knowledge about the Bible, but there's no life in it. **The Bible is not an end but a stimulus to our interaction with God.**

Though we read God's Word, we're not feeding on God. Start with a conscious desire to engage Him in a personal way. Select a portion of Scripture—a verse, a paragraph, a chapter—and read it over and over. Think of Him as present and speaking to you, disclosing His mind and emotions and will. God is articulate: He speaks to us through His Word.

Meditate on His words until **God's thoughts begin to take shape in your mind.** "Thoughts" is exactly the right word because that's precisely what the Bible is — *"the mind of the Lord"* (**1 Corinthians 2:16**). When we read His Word, we are reading His mind—what He knows, what He feels, what He wants, what He enjoys, what He desires, what He loves, what He hates.

Deep within us is a place for God. Take time to reflect on what He is saying. Think about each word. Give yourself time for prayerful contemplation until God's heart is revealed and your heart is exposed. From time to time, make short pauses to allow these truths time to flow through all the recesses of the soul.

Listen carefully to the words that touch your emotions and meditate on His goodness. "*Feed on His faithfulness*" (**Psalm 37:3**). Think about His kindness and those glimpses of His unfailing love that motivates you to love Him more (**Psalm 48:9**). Savor His words. "*Taste and see that the Lord is good*" (**Psalm 34:8**). Start with a conscious desire to engage Him in a personal way.

Maybe you were expecting Him to talk to you in an audible voice, but **God did speak to you through your pastor's sermon**. But you didn't hear because you weren't paying attention. That doesn't mean that the Lord is silent, but you were distracted by your problems, your pending tasks, or other little things. So, pay attention. Maybe He is not silent at all.

Listen to God's voice in your circumstances. Sometimes we focus too much on our situations, and we say that God is silent because we cannot hear Him. However, we need to learn to notice His voice through what He is doing in our lives. Sometimes the answer to our prayers comes through events instead of actual words (**Acts 16:6–7**).

Learn to discern whether it was God's voice, someone else's, or your imagination. Our eagerness or inexperience may trick us into thinking that we've heard the voice of God when it wasn't so. That's why you need to distinguish the desires of your heart and God's desire for your life. Therefore, you need to learn more about God and His will from the

Bible – He won't speak something to us that doesn't agree with Scripture. The more you learn, the more you can discern (**Hebrews 5:14**).

During Jesus's ministry on earth, many people followed Him to gain something from Him, not because of Him (**John 6:26**). Don't make the same mistake! Seek Him with the genuine desire to know Him. Seek Him for who He is, and you will hear His voice, whatever way He chooses to speak to you (**Proverbs 3:5–6**).

Christ Jesus is the Living Word of God (**John 1:1,14**). He is the answer to our most urgent prayer: the prayer for forgiveness of our sins so we can have access to God. The good news is that thanks to the blood of Jesus, this is within our reach by God's grace through faith in Him (**Ephesians 2:8–9**). The important truth is that God spoke to all of us through His Son and through Scripture. **Be grateful that, because of Jesus, you were also given access to the Father and a hearing heart through the Holy Spirit's presence in you.**

If you struggle with talking with God in your daily journey, I recommend using a simple shoe leather method of prayer that is called "ACTS":

- **A**doration: Give God praise and honor for who He is as Lord over all creation.

- **C**onfession: Honestly deal with the sin in your life. To confess is to agree with God about your missing the mark.

- **T**hanksgiving: Verbalize what you're grateful for in your life and in the world around you. God loves hearing "Thank You" even in things we don't understand and appear negative to us.

- **S**upplication: Pray for the needs of others and yourself.

Then listen to God.

"If you aren't active in your prayer life, think about what you could be missing out on. Think about the mysteries and answers that God isn't revealing to you simply because you aren't asking and calling on God. Prayer is the line that connects. 'Continue earnestly in prayer, being vigilant in it with thanksgiving.' **(Colossians 4:2)"** — **John Grant,** chairman of America's Board of the United Bible Societies

---

SOME PERSONAL STEPS IN SHOE LEATHER

I think sometimes I have tried to make prayer a responsibility instead of an intimate opportunity. I know that God (like any father) doesn't desire a repetition and structured conversation with Him. He is my Heavenly Father who desires that I love Him and acknowledge Him in everything, big or small. He desires that we speak from the heart in truth and reality. He already knows my thoughts and wants me to be intimate with Him, so I mentally and sometimes verbally acknowledge and share all that is in my mind with Him. **Prayer is an intimate connection with God, who created me and loves me more than any human can.**

Also, I understand what 1 Thessalonians **5:17** says *"Pray without ceasing."* This doesn't mean I need to have my head bowed, hands folded, and eyes closed all day long. (Look out, Houston drivers, if I did that.) No, this means to me that God and I have open-ended conversations; these prayers have no end and are open for either God or me to jump back in.

My sons and I get together on a regular basis to pray about our businesses which our primary business for many years has been discount prescriptions. This has virtually dried up during and after the COVID crisis. Our other business is in wastewater evaporation with a new patented technology that has taken ten years to develop and pass all the various state regulations. We are just now getting a significant acceleration in that business. We know God owns our businesses, so we strive to include Him in our business decisions.

My wife of 55 years had struggled for thirteen years in her fight against cancer, the last two being the hardest. After years of prayer, she finally got her heart's desire to go Home to Heaven. But God allowed her to lead many to Christ, including her brother, along the path of her cancer journey and her many prayers for others.

God has been with us every step of the way and has made Himself very evident in these earthly struggles. God has made it clear to us that He wants to be involved in everything, big or small. He has made it clear that He is in control and wants us to thank Him for everything, regardless of our feelings or circumstances.

We have truly come to realize that our Heavenly Father loves us immensely and wants us to talk with Him continuously if nothing more than a quick "Thank You" several times throughout the day.

CHAPTER 7.
THINKING LIKE JESUS

"A biblical worldview is thinking like Jesus. It is a way of making our faith practical to every situation we face each day. A biblical worldview is a way of dealing with the world such that we act like Jesus twenty-four hours a day because we think like Jesus." — **George Barna**, in his book "Think Like Jesus."

Our ever-present traveling companion, the Holy Spirit, desires to conform us to the image of Jesus Christ (**Romans 8:29**). This primarily means He wants to help us to think like Jesus because, as **Proverbs 23:7** informs us of the reality, *"As a man thinks, so is he."*

One of the most amazing gifts that God has given us is the human mind. The ability to learn, think, choose, and reason is the essence of what makes us human. While the ability to think makes us human, it actually goes deeper. Your thoughts become a reflection of who you really are. Thoughts come into our minds; then we act on those thoughts; actions are done over and over, become habits that then become a major part of our lifestyle and determine how we see and comprehend all the various issues in the world.

The mind is neutral. It depends on what is put into it to determine which way it will go. The expression, "Garbage in, garbage out," is true. You have two major influences on your mind. God, who loves us and wants the best for us, wants us to yield to the control of the indwelling Holy Spirit to control our thoughts for us to have the mind of Christ with Godly wisdom with an eternal perspective. The second major influence is focused on the flesh and this world and comes either directly or indirectly from Satan and his demonic followers, who can produce a carnal mind in any number of ways with human and worldly wisdom with a temporal perspective.

So, basically, a believer in Jesus Christ has a choice of two thought alternatives—the mind of Christ or a carnal mind.

As Paul informs us in **1 Corinthians 2: 9—16** that God's wisdom is revealed through the mind of Christ to believers by the Holy Spirit *"What no eye has seen, what no ear has heard, and what no human mind has conceived the things God has prepared for those who love Him—these are the things God has revealed to us by His Spirit. The Spirit searches all things, even the deep things of God. For who knows a person's thoughts except for their own spirit within them? In the same way, no one knows the thoughts of God except the Spirit of God. What we have received is not the spirit of the world, but the Spirit who is from God, so that we may understand what God has freely given us. This is what we speak, not in words taught us by human wisdom but in words taught by the Spirit, explaining spiritual realities with Spirit-taught words. The person without the Spirit does not accept the things that come from the Spirit of God but considers them foolishness and cannot understand them because they are discerned only through the Spirit. The person with the Spirit makes judgments about all things, but such a person is* *not subject to merely human judgments, for, Who has known the mind of the Lord to instruct him? But we have the mind of Christ."*

One of Satan's primary tactics is to influence our thoughts. We are being invaded by Satan and his demon army in the world today with this battle tactic of controlling our thoughts. During my life, I have been a witness to what has appeared to be a growing trend of evil. However, from reading the Old Testament, this evil trend has been here since Adam and Eve disobeyed God. Immediately after this fall, brother was killing brother, and evil progressed and flourished until every person was doing what was right in their own eyes.

I have concluded that we have two major differences now that did not exist in both Old and New Testament times: 1) a human population of almost eight billion which is at least twenty-four times larger than New Testament times, with only 31% identifying as Christians, and 2) instant communication digital devices connecting the whole earth, even in the most remote and impoverished areas. In 2022 91.54% of people worldwide (7.26 billion) owned a cell phone, and 86% of the population owned a smartphone with an integrated computer and internet access. As of April 2022, there were five billion internet users worldwide, and this is expected to increase to six billion in 2023. The typical global internet user spends almost seven hours per day using the internet, which is about 40% of their waking time. The latest calculations suggest that the world spent more than 12 ½ trillion hours online in 2022.

Now if you were Satan and you were limited by being created without the omniscience of God, and you can only be in one place at a time, the same being true of your demon (fallen created angels) followers, where would you make your spiritual attack on humans to have the most impact? The obvious answer is controlling the content on media (including the internet, news reporting, television, radio, social media, etc.), in education (from preschool through college), in governments, in politics, in sports, in entertainment, and in every other arena of influence. In order to control the content, all Satan has to do is control the thoughts of the relatively few numbers of people who have authority over the decisions made in those arenas of influence.

How successful has Satan been? All you have to do is check the internet, watch television, go to the movies, read newspapers, hear the teachings in schools, etc., to see a growing prevalence of antibiblical, antichrist, and Satanic content that negatively affects the world with evil and fear.

Fear is allowing someone or something to control you. That is why we are told to fear only God. (Psalm 31:19,111:10, Exodus 20:20, 2 Cor. 5:11) All kinds of good will flow into the life of the person who fears the Lord and yields to His control. All kinds of evil flow into the life of a person who allows Satan to control him/her through his/her thoughts.

The entire realm of unbelieving humanity lies under the binding influence of the evil one. *"The whole world lies under the sway of the wicked one"* **(1 John 5:19)**. Even those unbelievers who do not accept the truths of God about Satan and sin are nonetheless captivated by him. Consequently, we are to humbly reach out to them with the truth: *"In humility correcting those who are in opposition, if God perhaps will grant them repentance, so that they may know the truth, and that they may come to their senses and escape the snare of the devil, having been taken captive by him to do his will."* **(2 Timothy 2:26)**

Paul was sent forth to proclaim the gospel truth that offers freedom from such bondage: *"to open their eyes and to turn them from darkness to light, and from the power of Satan to God"* (**Acts 26:18**). The testimony of all who believe in the **truth of the gospel is this: *"He (God) has delivered us from the power of darkness and translated us into the kingdom of the Son of His love"* (Colossians 1:13).**

The problem of Satan's binding, hindering, and restricting influence does not end with our acceptance of Christ as our salvation. Many saints (though headed for heaven, are spiritual babies) are still bound in areas of their thinking and behavior. They are still influenced by the enemy's lies. They cannot make the liberating confession of Paul and his missionary team *"We are not ignorant of his* [Satan's] *devices"* (**2 Corinthians 2:11**). Ignorance of the enemy's tactics will persist in the lives of those who do not know (or will not yield to) God's liberating truth.

God has provided an offensive weapon for each of us to fight these ongoing battles of spiritual warfare in **Ephesians 6:17** *"…the sword of the Spirit, which is the Word of God."* All who are willing to embrace the truths of God's Word will enjoy more and more freedom from the enemy's lies. Jesus states in **John 8:31—32** *"If you continue in my word, you are truly my disciples and you will know the truth, and the truth will set you free."* They will grow in understanding of, and reliance upon, the victorious purposes of Jesus' coming to this earth. *"For this purpose, the Son of God was manifested that He might destroy the works of the devil"* (**1 John 3:8**).

The war against Satan and his followers has already been won at the cross. Satan's demise is already written by His Creator in **Revelation 20:10**

"And the devil that deceived them was cast into the lake of fire...and shall be tormented day and night forever and ever." **Do not fear him; Satan's ongoing battles to control your thoughts today can be defeated with the powerful and living Word of God.**

BELIEVER'S CHOICE OF TWO THOUGHT ALTERNATIVES
(YIELDING TO THE CONTROL OF THE HOLY SPIRIT)

(Col 3:2)	(2 Cor 10:3-5)		
MIND OF CHRIST →	OBEDIENCE- →	FRUIT OF →	ABUNDANT LIFE &
(God's wisdom and	LOVE GOD &	THE SPIRIT	PEACE (TRANSFORMED
understanding; Holy	OTHERS	(John 15:4-5,8)	INTO CHRIST'S
Spirit reveals these)	(Phil 2:2-5)		IMAGE)
(1 Cor 2:9-16)	(James 3:17)		
(James 1:5)			

⬈ (Rom 7:25-8:8)	(Prov 23:7)	(Gal 5:16-26)	(Rom 8:6)
THOUGHTS →	ACTIONS →	HABITS →	LIFESTYLE
⬊ (Eph 4:17-24)	(Luke 6:45)	(Luke 6:43)	
(James 1:8)			

CARNAL MIND →	DISOBEDIENCE →	LUST of EYE →	DEATH-
(Human and worldly	LOVE SELF &	LUST of FLESH	(SEPARATION)
wisdom; flesh or	WORLD	PRIDE of LIFE	
demons reveal these)	(Mat 15:18-19)	(1 John 2:16)	
(1 Cor 3:1-3)	(James 3:14-16)		

CONTRAST BETWEEN THE MIND OF CHRIST AND THE CARNAL MIND

THE MIND OF CHRIST

THE CARNAL MIND

Disciplined (Spiritual breathing; **John 13:4-10** Foot washing; **Eph5:18** Filling of Holy Spirit)

Undisciplined (Allow emotions to control life; baby maturity—ME)

Proactive (Wants to bring God pleasure)	**Lazy** (Brings God grief)
Eternal view (God owns everything— possessions, health, relationships, etc.)	**Temporal view** (I own everything)
God is in control (He is sovereign)	**I am in control** (Captain of my own destiny)
Giving (I am God's steward)	**Getting** (One dollar more)
Significance-oriented	**Success-oriented**
Listens to heart	**Listens to head**
Unconditional love (Based on grace)	**Conditional love** (Based on performance)
Relationship-based (John 17:3 Knowing God and developing intimacy)	**Self-based**
Servant leader	**Self-serving leader**
Audience of One (Matthew 25:21)	**Audience of the world** (I'm No. 1)
Purpose-driven (God has a plan for each of us)	**Self-driven** (instant gratification, recognition, power/status)

EGO—Exalting God Only   **EGO—Edging God Out** (Pride)

Trusts God only (Proverbs 3:5, 6)   **Trusts in Self or Something Else (Psalms 118:8)**

Take Every Thought Captive

So, we must deal very carefully with our thoughts since they basically control us. In fact, God tells us that we must take every thought captive.

*"For though we live in the world, we do not wage war as the world does. The weapons we fight with are not the weapons of the world. On the contrary, they have the divine power to demolish strongholds. We demolish arguments and every pretension that sets itself up against the knowledge of God, and **we take captive every thought to make it obedient to Christ.**"* **(2 Corinthians 10:3—5)**

Here are a few ways to take our thoughts captive:

1.   Exercise our mind.

Just as we exercise our physical body to remain physically fit, we need to exercise our minds to be spiritually fit. In the New Testament, we have the Greek word, '**Phroneo,**' which, in essence, means "to exercise your mind."

*"For they that are after the flesh do **PHRONEO** the things of the flesh; but they that are after the Spirit do **PHRONEO** the things of the Spirit. For to be carnally **PHRONEMA** (minded=result of exercise) is spiritual death, but to*

*be spiritually, **PHRONEMA** is life and peace. The carnal **PHRONEMA** is enmity against God...."* **(Romans 8:5—7).**

The very best way to exercise our minds is to be in God's Word on a disciplined basis. Just as we schedule times to "exercise our physical body," we must have the same discipline to schedule times to "exercise our mind."

2.   Ask. Is this thought pleasing to God?

"Do not be conformed to this present world but be you transformed by the renewing of your mind, so that you may test and approve what is the will of God—what is good and well-pleasing and perfect." **(Romans 12:2)**

The word **"transformed"** is the Greek word **"metamorphosis,"** which is what happens when a caterpillar spins a web, then struggles out of the web to become a beautiful butterfly. You no longer have to be a creature slowly moving through a difficult world but one with wings to fly above it. You are then able to *"Set your mind on things above, not on the things of earth."* **(Colossians 3:2)**

3.   Ask. Can I be thankful to God for this thought?

"In everything give thanks, for this is the will of God in Christ Jesus concerning you." **(1 Thessalonians 5:18)**

A loving Father (both our earthly and Heavenly) always loves to hear, "Thank You," but in most cases, would question our thanking Him for something sinful and evil. Probably would reveal that we have an unhealthy love for the world also. *"Such a person is double-minded and unstable in all they do."* **(James 1:8)**

Instead, we should be praying that God delivers us from evil or, like Joseph told his brothers who had many years in the past sold him into slavery, that God uses this evil in a Genesis 50:20 eternally significant way, *"But as for you, you meant evil against me; but God meant it for good, in order to bring it about as it is this day, to save many people alive."* For this, we should be thankful.

4. Take our disabling thoughts captive through confession.

Confront our disabling thoughts. Turn them over to God and become who He sees we can be. It will take work to take our thoughts captive *each time* they pop into our minds. But it is possible with the help of the indwelling Holy Spirit.

5. Choose to focus our thoughts on the right things.

"Finally, brothers and sisters, whatever is true, whatever is noble, whatever is right, whatever is pure, whatever is lovely, whatever is admirable— if anything is excellent or praiseworthy—think about such things." **(Philippians 4:8)**

When we think about those things, God promises to give us His peace **(Philippians 4:9)**. What a contrast that is to the thoughts of millions of people today. Don't wrongly expect a movie, a TV show, social media, or how-to formula to accomplish this for you. It takes personal discipline and commitment.

6. Ask. What would Jesus do?

Before taking any action on a thought, ask this simple question. Our aim will be to act just as He would if He were in our place, regardless of immediate results. In other words, we propose to follow Jesus' steps as closely and as literally as we believe He taught His disciples to do.

Additional Verses on the Mind of Christ and Thinking like Jesus.

These verses from God's Word will provide some good concluding statements:

"If you are guided by the Spirit, you won't obey your selfish desires. The Spirit and your desires are enemies of each other. They are always fighting each other and keeping you from doing what you feel you should. But if you obey the Spirit, the Law of Moses has no control over you. People's desires make them give in to immoral ways, filthy thoughts, and shameful deeds. They worship idols, practice witchcraft, hate others, and are hard to get along with. People become jealous, angry, and selfish. They not only argue and cause trouble, but they are envious. They get drunk, carry on at wild parties, and do other evil things as well. I told you before, and I am telling you again: No one who does these things will share in the blessings of God's kingdom. God's Spirit makes us loving, happy, peaceful, patient, kind, good, faithful, gentle, and self-controlled. There is no law against behaving in any of these ways. And because we belong to Christ Jesus, we have killed our selfish feelings and desires. God's Spirit has given us life, and so we should follow the Spirit. But don't be conceited or make others jealous by claiming to be better than they are." **(Galatians 5:16—26)**

"In the Lord's name, I tell you this. Do not continue living like those who do not believe. Their thoughts are worth nothing. They do not understand, and they know nothing because they refuse to listen. So, they cannot have the life that God gives. They have lost all feelings of shame, and they use their lives for doing evil. They continually want to do all kinds of evil. But what you learned

in Christ was not like this. I know that you heard about him, and you are in him, so you were taught the truth that is in Jesus. You were taught to leave your old self—to stop living the evil way you lived before. That old self becomes worse because people are fooled by the evil things they want to do. But you were taught to be made new in your hearts, to become a new person. That new person is made to be like God—made to be truly good and holy." **(Ephesians 4:17—24)**

"Fulfill you my joy, that you be like-minded, have the same love, being of one accord of one mind. Let nothing be done through strife or vainglory, but in lowliness of mind, let each esteem others better than themselves. Look not every man on his own things, but every man also on the things of others. Let this mind be in you, which is also in Christ Jesus." **(Philippians 2:2—5)**

"I do not know where Thinking Like Jesus Thinks might lead us. I imagine we will be led to some uncomfortable circumstances. But if you want to take your Christian faith seriously, you will have to strive to have the same mind in you that is in Christ Jesus. You must endeavor to Think Like Jesus Thinks. Self-ambition, conceit, pride, arrogance, looking to your own interest—these are the thoughts of men. Humility and unconditional love are the thoughts of God. Think not of your own interest but also of the interests of others. Think Like Jesus." **Rev. Frank Logue,** sermon on "Thinking Like Jesus Thinks."

SOME PERSONAL STEPS IN SHOE LEATHER

In my business and personal situations, I have had and have negative things happening. In the early 1990s, I was on the verge of bankruptcy, and this went on for years before resolution. In 2009 my wife was diagnosed with nonsmoker's lung cancer involving thirteen years of surgeries, chemotherapy, and radiation treatments with no physical healing.

I have found through years of experience and walking with Jesus that He allows me the choice of thoughts about these negative happenings. I can be swayed by the world and my anxiety to let these negative circumstances control my thinking, or I can take every thought captive to the glory of God. I know, through these and other personal experiences, my loving Heavenly Father truly is behind the scenes doing what is eternally best for me.

I have chosen to think like Jesus and have an eternal perspective. This has allowed me to be thankful for all things, even those with tremendous pain and suffering.

CHAPTER 8.
DOING GREATER THINGS

"God is preparing you for greater things." **Curt Landry**, Messianic Jewish minister

"Greater things are yet to come; greater things are still to be done here." **Chris Tomlin,** Christian singer and worship leader

As we journey through life with God, He provides believers the power to do supernatural, eternally significant things. The night before Jesus was crucified, He made a dramatic statement recorded in **John 14:12, "***Very truly I tell you, whoever believes in me will do the works I have been doing, and they will do even **greater things** than these because I am going to the Father."*

This is an astonishing promise to all believers then and now. It does not exclude any Christian believer. It isn't just for pastors, or veteran Christians, or highly spiritual, mature Christians, or professional Christians, or missionaries, or elders, or evangelists, or highly gifted Christians. Jesus says, *"Whoever believes in me."* Believers, pure and simple, will do the works Jesus did. This should be the normal striving of every believer.

So, whatever the specific works are that Jesus has in mind, what defines them here is that they point to Jesus, which helps people believe in him. They are a witness to Jesus' words that lead people to faith. In **John 10:25,** Jesus underlines this fact, "*The works I do in my Father's name are a witness for me,*" That's what his works do, and he is saying, at least, that's what all believers' works do. "*Whoever believes in me will do the works I do*" — the works that point people to faith. If you are a believer in Jesus, that's what your life is. Your works and your life are a display of the trustworthiness of Jesus.

In His prayer in **John 17**, Jesus prayed, "*Father, I glorified You on earth, having accomplished the work that You gave Me to do.*" His *work* was what He did to draw attention to the glory of His Father. In **John 13:35,** Jesus said, "*By this, all people will know that you are my disciples if you have love for one another.*" A life of *love* will draw attention to the truth of Christ and the reality of our own new life in Him.

And in **Matthew 5:16,** Jesus said, "*Let your light shine before others, so that they may see your good works and give glory to your Father who is in heaven.*" **Christians are defined by works or life which flow from faith in Jesus and point to the glory of Jesus.** "*For we are His workmanship, created in Christ Jesus for good works, which God prepared beforehand that we should walk in them*" (**Ephesians 2:10**).

The idea that anyone could do **"greater" works** than Jesus is unfathomable. The New Testament not only relates divine miracles such as control over nature and weather (**Mark 4:38–40**), walking on water (**Matthew 14:25**), feeding 5,000 families with two fish and five loaves (**Matthew 14:16–21**), and raising the dead (**John 11:43–44**). It credits Him with creation itself

(**John 1:1–3**). In terms of power, it's logically impossible to suggest anyone could do something beyond what Jesus accomplished. The meaning, therefore, ought to be taken in some other way.

After Jesus' resurrection and forty days on earth, and just prior to His ascension to His Father, He gave a promise to the disciples then and to us now, recorded in **Acts 1:8**, *"But you will receive power when the Holy Spirit comes on you, and you will be my witnesses in Jerusalem, and in all Judea and Samaria, and to the ends of the earth."* And in the power of that absolutely new experience — the indwelling of the crucified and risen Christ — your works of love and your message of life in union with Christ will point people to the glory of the risen Son of God, and you will be the instrument of their forgiveness on the basis of the finished work of Christ (**John 20:22–23**).

What are the **great things** that any believer could do? It is to share the Gospel with someone so that they might be saved. Naturally, God does the saving, and it's not our responsibility to save anyone. It is their response to His ability, but it is our responsibility to share the good news with lost people in the hopes that God grants them repentance (**2 Timothy 2:25**).

If God uses us to heal someone by praying for them, that's great…all glory to God, but to have someone healed while still rejecting the Gospel means they'll only live a healthier life on their way to hell. What is greater than rescuing a person who would otherwise perish apart from Christ? Does healing sickness or disease equal eternal life in Christ? No way! That's greater than any physical healing, isn't it? Even self-proclaimed faith healers die…but Jesus said, *"Whoever believes in me, though he dies, yet shall he live"* (**John 11:25**).

You can be healed by a miracle and still die in your sins, but when a person puts their trust in Christ, they can endure in this life, even if they're never healed. They know that not even death can separate them from the love of God (**Romans 8:38–39**). They also understand that God uses suffering for His glory and their best. We are refined by being passed through the flames yet not tossed into the fire. *"For the message of the cross is foolishness to those who are perishing, but to us who are being saved it is the power of God."* (**1 Corinthians 1:18**)

To do great things, we use the power of God of His Good News of salvation from eternal separation from God through the finished work of Christ on the cross.

So, it becomes obvious that the area of "greater things" where Christian believers can exceed what Jesus did is not "quality" but "quantity." His earthly ministry lasted only about three years and was restricted to foot travel, mainly through Israel. Jesus preached without modern communications or modern travel availabilities. In contrast, current technology tools, such as smartphones and the internet, allow the gospel to be shared with millions worldwide. Modern evangelists can preach to hundreds of thousands of people on television, YouTube, and social media. Missionaries can serve the furthest reaches of the globe with Bibles translated into the native tongues of almost every language.

Fifty days after Christ's resurrection, just ten days after Christ ascended into Heaven, God fulfilled His promise in **Acts 1:8** and sent the Holy Spirit to indwell believers with the Holy Spirit to be Christ's witnesses. The Apostle Peter, who was by himself so weak, timid, and powerless, was filled with boldness and power when the Holy Spirit took control of his life! In his Pentecostal sermon, Peter does his first **"greater quantity things than Christ"** when 3,000 people accept Jesus Christ as their Savior. Peter is one of the greatest examples that we have of a life transformed by God through the power of the Holy Spirit.

Yes, we are human beings with all the related tendencies and weaknesses. But we don't have to be bound by this! These are not actually the things that dictate how our lives will go. God gives the Holy Spirit to all who obey Him **(Acts 5:32).** If we walk in the Spirit and live in obedience to His promptings, we will receive all the power in heaven and on earth to carry out God's good and perfect will for our lives. We will be driven by the same powerful engine that worked such a remarkable transformation in Peter and allowed him to do greater things in quantity than Jesus.

"Today, we're able to reach even greater audiences than they could. We have greater technology and can reach more people than Jesus or the apostles could, but if they mean that they are doing greater miracles than Jesus, they don't understand the context of Jesus' sayings. Besides, I believe that the greatest miracle for us was our conversion. God can and still is doing miracles, I am sure, but what greater thing is there than to be used by God to rescue the perishing from the gates of hell and bring them into the kingdom by the Word of God and the Spirit of God, and all for the glory of God." — **Jack Wellman,** Christian author and pastor

---

SOME PERSONAL STEPS IN SHOE LEATHER

In my years on earth, I have had the awesome thrills to watch God through the power of His Holy Spirit using ordinary weak, timid, and

powerless "Peters" of today to do greater things "in quantity" than Jesus. A few of the ones that God allowed me the privilege of personally knowing and being involved with them in their "**greater things**" include:

(1) Bill Bright was born near the small town of Coweta, Okla., in 1921 to a cattle ranching dad and a school teaching mother. Bright attended a one-room schoolhouse until the eighth grade. After graduating with honors from Oklahoma's Northeastern State University in 1944, Bright moved to Southern California and began a successful confectionery company.

In 1951, Bright says he was inspired to leave his budding business empire and embrace the scriptural command to "go and make disciples of all the nations" (**Matthew 28:19**). In 1951, Bill Bright pursued his passion for ministry by starting **Campus Crusade for Christ (CRU)** at the University of California, Los Angeles.

In 1979, Bill Bright and CRU introduced The JESUS Film, a feature-length documentary on the life of Christ. The JESUS Film and its translation into other languages were developed and were initially used solely inside of CRU. This film, based on the Gospel of Luke, from 1979 through mid-2023, has been translated into 2,033 languages and has had more than 10.5 billion viewings worldwide, which has resulted through mid-2023 in **633 million indicated decisions to follow Christ**. It has become the largest evangelistic tool that God has provided, where at the average showing, 10% of the viewers decide to follow Christ.

(2) Walt Wilson went into the fledgling technology business in 1960 after serving as a Sergeant in the US Marine Corps for four years. Early in his career Walt joined Apple when it was a startup.

After forty-five years of experience as an operating executive in Silicon Valley in three Fortune 50 companies, Walt founded **Global Media Outreach (GMO)** in 2004. GMO has become the world's leader in worldwide online evangelism in fifty languages reaching about 400,000 people daily with 50,000 indicated decisions daily. Since 2004 GMO has had in excess of 2.5 billion gospel visits, with over **278 million indicated decisions for Christ**.

(3) **Jerry Jackson** graduated with a Bachelor of Science in Agronomy degree from California State Polytechnic and managed an avocado packing house in Santa Paula, California, before entering full-time ministry in 1967. That year Jerry, Anet (his wife), and their four kids bought a school bus which they used as their home to travel from town to town, serving as itinerant missionaries in the western U.S. before settling in Albuquerque, New Mexico.

In 1972 they founded **Faith Comes By Hearing** (then named Hosanna) as a tape-lending ministry. Through the power of God, it progressed to be a champion for the unique needs of non-literate communities and has helped to pioneer many strategies for making Scripture available in a language and format people can best use. God has used this ministry to produce audio (many are dramatized) versions of the Bible.

In partnership with more than 700 organizations, Faith Comes By Hearing, as of mid-2023, has recorded Scripture in more than 1,800 languages and adapted 1,200+ Gospel films, freely making available **God's Word in audio and video for over 80% of the world's population**.

(4) **Ivan Bychkov and Sergey Khripunov** from Uzbekistan, a former socialist republic in the Soviet Union, were led to Christ by **Victoria**

Khripunov, wife of Sergey and the sister of Ivan. She had accepted Christ through watching The Jesus Film. Subsequently, God filled them with a Great Commission passion. They became beekeepers to smuggle Bibles using beehives into the country. Eventually, they were caught, thrown into jail, and then they and their families were thrown out of Uzbekistan. They did not know what God planned next for them. God, in His sovereignty, introduced them to a businessman from Houston who helped their families move to Houston.

In a short time, the two, with some family members, started a sports program, initially a soccer program for refugees in Houston, and used that platform to share the Gospel of Christ. God expanded this program, **Sports Catalyst**, rapidly, and it moved to other cities and then to other countries, involving other sports. Currently, it is in **over 200 countries in the world**.

Recently, God used these two men and Sports Catalyst to lead a humanitarian effort to set up 119 aid centers in countries around Ukraine to help many of the millions of refugees fleeing the conflict there, once again, focused on sharing the Gospel and love of Christ. In my wife Wanda's going home celebration, these two men plus their spouses were seated by the ushers next to someone in another ministry they did not know, Morgan Jackson. God used that coincidence (God happening) to form a partnership between Faith Comes by Hearing (FCBH) and Sports Catalyst, whereby the military Ukrainians would each be provided a Bible audio listening device. Already tens of thousands have been provided by FCBH and distributed by Sports Catalyst.

In each of these ordinary people's cases, and in dozens of others with which I am personally familiar, **God uses the ripple effect to work "greater things." The ordinary person has a small pebble of faith that he or**

she tosses into the lake of divine opportunities, and God in His power causes ripple effects that continue to ripple into "greater things."

I am convinced that God wants to use each follower of Christ in even larger supernatural ways to be involved in "greater things" that none of us can even begin to imagine. Through our faith, we must allow God in His power to direct our every step to where He is working so that we can join Him. In each of the four ministries previously mentioned, God is obviously "at work in greater things," and I wanted to join Him there.

Let me encourage you as an ordinary believer to step boldly out in weakness and in faith with great expectation to join God where He is working, expecting Him to do greater things.

God truly desires to continue to use each ordinary believer to be involved in greater things in his/her individual Shoe Leather Journey.

"Many Christians estimate difficulty in the light of their own resources and thus they attempt very little, and they always fail. All giants have been weak men who did great things for God because they reckoned on His power and presence to be with them." ---**J. Hudson Taylor,** British missionary

CHAPTER 9.
BRAGGING ON JESUS (WITNESSING)

"Let him who boasts (brags), boast (brag) on the Lord" (**1 Corinthians 1:31**).

Bragging or boasting about someone or something is almost a daily activity for us. When you are a parent or grandparent, it is almost impossible not to brag about your kids or grandkids. Social media, such as Facebook and Instagram, makes this bragging even easier to share with your friends.

Almost all businesses use many marketing and advertising strategies and techniques to use this inborn human activity of bragging to sell their products and services. Bragging is nothing more than "endorsing" something or someone. Highly recognized athletes in almost every sport and other celebrities are paid millions of dollars every year to endorse or say something good about products or services. It is a genuine wonder in our world today that people would buy something based on what someone else says about it. But...

How about that good movie that we just saw? How about that good restaurant in which we ate? How about my team? We enjoy saying good things about something or someone that has brought us enjoyment and pleasure.

This is exactly what Jesus has asked us to do—say something good about Him to others, brag about Him, and tell others how much joy He brings you.

"Do you want to brag? Brag on Jesus. Forget self-exaltation. Get into God-exaltation. Get into Christ-exaltation, and you can boast all you want." — **John Piper,** American theologian

Jesus basically commissions all his disciples, including future ones, with the job of telling others about Jesus. This Great Commission that Jesus gave the disciples and us is recorded in **Acts 1:8,** *"But you shall receive power when the Holy Spirit has come upon you, and you shall be my witnesses in Jerusalem, and in all Judea and Samaria, and to the ends of the earth."*

The Great Commission has two parts to it—the disciples' (our) responsibility or job and God's provision to help them (us) do that job.

Jesus said that the disciples' job then and our responsibility now are to be witnesses of Jesus, no matter where we are. This is a command and not a choice. What is a witness? Webster's Dictionary defines a <u>witness</u> as "one who gives testimony." Basically, a witness gives the <u>facts of his/her story</u>.

Witnessing or giving testimony or telling your story involves only facts as you know them. If you are subpoenaed to be a witness in a courtroom, you are restricted from giving hearsay. You must deal only with facts as you know them. So, witnessing is very personal, and the facts of your witness are personal to you. No one can dispute facts that only you have. This certainly helps us not to feel so pressured when no one can question our facts relating to our individual stories.

What are the reasons that we do not witness or brag about Jesus? Fear is the basis for most of the reasons—fear of rejection, fear of ridicule, fear of not having enough Biblical knowledge, fear of not knowing what to say, fear of failure, etc. Fear is allowing someone or something to control you. That is why God tells us to fear only Him; let Him alone control us.

This fear of witnessing can be removed by completely understanding what Jesus said in **Acts 1:8**. The awesome part of this verse is that God knows that witnessing is hard and difficult for a believer, so He wants to be directly involved by providing His power to you. He truly wants to use ordinary people to do extraordinary things. Some realizations about the power of God available to us, when we witness, should aid in reducing the pressure of witnessing.

When we do our job of witnessing, God's power through the Holy Spirit becomes available in unfathomable ways. The night before Jesus was crucified, he was teaching the disciples about the coming of the Holy Spirit, as is recorded in **John chapters 14–17. John 14:12** that we studied in the previous chapter on "Doing Greater Things" presents the exciting truth of God's power available to believers. And **Ephesians 3:20** adds further excitement, "*Now to Him (refers to God) who can do exceedingly abundantly beyond all that we ask or think, according to the power that works within us.*" Other verses in scripture point to the same basic principle—**When an ordinary person accepts Jesus Christ as his/her personal savior and is indwelled with the Holy Spirit, God desires to use that ordinary person to do extraordinary (greater) things through His indwelling power.**

Witnessing is how God allows us supernaturally to be involved in His redemption process. We are not asked by God to use our human power to put the hard sell on someone for Jesus. **We are asked by God not to be salespersons but to be satisfied customers. God is the only salesman needed.** In **John 6:44,** Jesus says that no man can come to Me except the Father draws him. In **John 16:8,** Jesus says that the Holy Spirit is the One that convinces each one of sin and righteousness and of judgment. In **1 Corinthians 3:6–7** Paul states that *"I have planted, Apollos watered, but God gave the increase. So then, neither the one who plants nor the one who waters is anything, but God who causes the increase."*

The story that is told in all four gospels about the feeding of the 5,000 wonderfully shows the interaction between God's power and a believer's involvement. In **John 6:1–13,** Jesus asks His disciples where to buy food for the entire massive crowd (5,000 men plus probably 5,000 women and 5,000 or more children). He was testing them to see if they would use God's power for the problem or their own human power. They immediately tried human power first by checking their money supply and found it inadequate. Next, they checked the food supply available in the crowd and found only a boy with two small fish and five loaves of bread. It quickly became clear that their human resources were vastly insufficient to meet the problem. So, Jesus took what little they had and multiplied it with God's power. Jesus asked them to distribute the food and round up the leftovers—a basket full for each of the twelve. **This story strongly shows us that all God wants of us is to bring what little we have, and He, in His power, will multiply it in Ephesians 3:20 ways.**

Our witnessing is sharing the little that we have with others and allowing God in His power to multiply it. It is like taking a small pebble and tossing it into the lake; the pebble has very little effect on the lake, but because of the pebble, a little ripple starts, then a slightly bigger ripple, and so on until a large ripple has reached the shore. In commanding that we be a witness for Jesus wherever we are, **God only expects us to toss a small pebble and allow His power to cause a ripple effect.** However, God's power becomes available in our witnessing only when we toss a small pebble. God definitely wants us involved.

Some shoe leather practical pebble tossing ways to have opportunities to be involved in bragging about Jesus and being a witness for Him include:

1) Pray that the Holy Spirit will give you the opportunity to witness and prepare the person to have an open heart.

2) Invite a friend to attend or watch church online or on TV with you. Have a follow-up discussion about their thoughts.

3) Ask someone how you can pray for them. Pray with them immediately, or text or email them a prayer if you are not physically with them.

4) Be a friend and a good listener.

5) Avoid arrogance and preachiness.

6) Text or email a note of Biblical encouragement.

7) Share what you read in your daily Bible reading and how it affected you.

8) *"In the same way, let your light shine before others so that they may see your good deeds and glorify your Father in heaven"* (**Matthew 5:16).**

"God's desire is for you to become a mouthpiece for Him." — **Jim Maxim**, Acts413 Ministries.

SOME PERSONAL STEPS IN SHOE LEATHER

On Facebook, I love to let my friends know what good things are happening to each member and extended member of my family. At the same time, I strive to include personal thanks, praise, or endorsement for God in each posting, realizing that He is more involved in their lives than I am. I also know that many of my friends throughout the world and the USA are not believers in Jesus Christ. Therefore, I want them to know how intimately involved my family, extended family, and I are with our Heavenly Father. I know that many of them will never go to a church to hear the truth about Jesus, but the Holy Spirit can speak to them even through social media.

One other thing that I do on social media, texting, and emailing, is to write my personal prayers for friends and acquaintances (believing and unbelieving) struggling with health or other issues. I start with "Heavenly Father" and end with "In Jesus' Name. Amen," I feel that this brings honor to God and probably comforts the recipient, even if not yet, a believer. The Holy Spirit may use it as a planted seed, as He does with most bragging and endorsement of God.

CHAPTER 10.
WHY ME, GOD?

"The pessimist sees difficulty in every opportunity. The optimist sees opportunity in every difficulty." — **Winston Churchill**

As we travel in our life journey with God, bad things happen to all of us. Most believers have the thought or openly express it— "WHY ME, GOD? We somehow mistakenly believe that since we have accepted Christ as our personal savior, He not only saves us spiritually for eternity, but He also saves us physically and mentally from the sufferings, pain, and problems of this fallen earth. When bad things happen, we become very upset and angry with our God, who we thought was our Heavenly Father, who loves us more than we love ourselves and wants the best for us (as we define it).

God allows us, as parents of children, to begin to see love from different perspectives. It somewhat helps us to see a little into God's perspective when we do not let our kids have their desires which we know may be the worst thing for them but usually causes emotional reactions from them because of our saying "No."

Our experiences of maturing as adults have taught us that our kids do crazy things for crazy reasons and expect the best, just like we did when we were kids. Some adults struggle with "growing up" and still react as kids. Anger, disappointment, and bitterness are the usual responses when things don't go as planned. Bitterness from both kids and adults can become very destructive in relationships.

Sports are a great way to teach hard lessons in life, particularly in discipline, hard work, teamwork, and humility. However, they can also teach bad lessons. In high school, we had a football team that did not win any games in my junior year. We worked as hard in practice as the teams that did win. In college, we had a change of head coach because of not winning. The new coach had the philosophy that torturous workouts would result in winning, which it didn't. It resulted in "running off" 127 out of 157 scholarship athletes, many of whom were our best players. Winning was the only proof of success, and it became a tremendously negative goal.

Our own experiences in parenting, sports, and other areas of our secular lives, however, do not provide an adequate foundation to journey through a life that has huge obstacles of bad things, problems, losses, failures, anger, pain, disappointment, and bitterness. We must add extra shoe leather (the Word of God) to help us trust that God is our loving Heavenly Father who truly does want the best for us.

As human beings, we are limited in our understanding of God. We live in a world of pain and suffering. There is no one who is not affected by the harsh realities of life, and the question "Why do bad things happen to good people?" is one of the most difficult questions in all of theology.

God is sovereign, so all that happens must have at least been allowed by Him, if not directly caused by Him. At the outset, we must acknowledge that human beings, who are not eternal, infinite, or omniscient, cannot expect to fully understand God's purposes and ways. Because we don't share those qualities with God, we can never fully understand all about what He is doing.

Why does God allow bad things to happen to good people?

To get a "little" insight into this question, it may be good to consider at least these thirteen things:

Bad things happen to good people, but:

1. This world is not the end.

Christians need to have an eternal perspective. We will have a reward someday, and it will be glorious. God tells us to keep our eyes on our eternal home as we travel on this brief trouble-filled, and painful journey because eternity is where our true glory comes.

"We do not lose heart. Though outwardly we are wasting away, inwardly, we are being renewed day by day. For our light and momentary troubles are achieving for us an eternal glory that far outweighs them all. So, we fix our eyes not on what is seen, but on what is unseen, since what is seen is temporary, but what is unseen is eternal" (**2 Corinthians 4:16–18**).

2. <u>God uses those bad things for eternally significant reasons.</u>

When Joseph, innocent of wrongdoing, was sold into slavery by his brothers, was wrongly placed into prison, and finally came through his thirteen years of suffering, he was finally able to see God's good plan in it all. God wants us to realize that He wants to use each of His children in **Genesis 50:20** ways for His salvation purposes.

"But as for you, you meant evil against me; but God meant it for good, in order to bring it about as it is this day, to save many people alive" **(Genesis 50:20).**

3. <u>Those bad things equip believers to help others through difficult situations.</u>

Those with battle scars can better help those going through battles.

"Praise be to . . . the Father of compassion and the God of all comfort, who comforts us in all our troubles so that we can comfort those in any trouble with the comfort we ourselves receive from God. For just as we share abundantly in the sufferings of Christ, so also our comfort abounds through Christ" **(2 Corinthians 1:3–5).**

"Bear one another's burdens, and so fulfill the law of Christ" **(Galatians 6:2).**

"One of the secrets of life is that all that is really worth doing is what we do for others." — **Lewis Carroll**, English author

4.   <u>Worse things happened to the Son of God.</u>

Jesus was the only truly Righteous One, yet He suffered more than we can imagine. We follow in His footsteps. Jesus is no stranger to our pain.

"If you suffer for doing good and you endure it, this is commendable before God. To this, you were called because Christ suffered for you, leaving you an example that you should follow in His steps. He committed no sin, and no deceit was found in His mouth. When they hurled their insults at Him, He did not retaliate; when He suffered, He made no threats. Instead, He entrusted Himself to Him who judges justly" (**1 Peter 2:20–23**).

5.   <u>These make us more Christlike.</u>

God is good, and His purposes for our lives, even in the difficult parts, are for our good. His ultimate goal is for us to become like Christ in our speech and actions. He has prepared works for us to do, all in line with His greater plans and purposes for the world. The trials and the temptations we face serve to shape us into people who are made in the image of Christ to accomplish His purposes.

"We know that in all things God works for the good of those who love Him, who have been called according to His purpose. For whom He foreknew, He also predestined to be conformed to the image of His Son, that He might be the firstborn among many brethren" (**Romans 8:28–29**).

6.   <u>These develop our character.</u>

There is a saying that hard things only serve to make us stronger. And that's true. God often uses the trials and temptations we face to change us. He has a vision of what He wants us to be. And sometimes, the person

He wants us to be can only be formed through the difficult situations that come into our lives.

"Not only that, but we rejoice in our sufferings, knowing that suffering produces endurance, and endurance produces character, and character produces hope, and hope does not put us to shame, because God's love has been poured into our hearts through the Holy Spirit who has been given to us" (**Romans 5:3–5**).

7.   These discipline us.

There are times when our own actions and attitudes are not in alignment with God's will and commandments. We often go astray, allow pride to rear its head, or forget to be kind to others. Sometimes God allows difficulties to arise because He wants to correct our hearts and souls to remind us of the need to walk in obedience to Him.

"My son, do not regard lightly the discipline of the Lord, nor be weary when reproved by him. For the Lord disciplines the one He loves and chastises every son whom He receives" (**Hebrews 12:5–6**).

8.   These test our faith.

God sometimes allows trials in our lives because He wants to test our faith for us to see if we are truly willing to follow Him no matter the cost. Though they can be indescribably difficult, we can stand firm and know that it will not last forever and that with His help, we can make it through.

"Count it all joy, my brothers, when you meet trials of various kinds, for you know that the testing of your faith produces steadfastness. And let steadfastness

have its full effect, that you may be perfect and complete, lacking in nothing" (**James 1:2–4**).

9. These help us grow in our faith.

When life is easy, it can be easy to become stagnant in our faith rather than grow and flourish. Hardships are used by God to get us out of our state of complacency and prompt us to grow up in the faith.

"And after you have suffered a little while, the God of all grace, who has called you to his eternal glory in Christ, will Himself restore, confirm, strengthen, and establish you" (**1 Peter 5:10**).

10. These help us to trust God alone.

There are times when we simply do not have all the answers, and the pain we feel from the difficult times in our lives does not make sense at all. We can be sure that even when it doesn't make sense to us, it does fit in God's perfect plans and purposes. Our job is to trust Him.

"Trust in the Lord with all your heart, and do not lean on your own understanding. In all your ways acknowledge him, and he will make straight your paths" (**Proverbs 3:5–6**).

11. There is power in failure.

Hebrews 11 is known as the Hall of Fame of Faith. It could also be called the Hall of Failures. Each person was an ordinary person who failed constantly. Abraham consistently lied; Noah drank too much; Jacob was a deceiver; Moses murdered a man; David was the cause of a man's murder, and he committed adultery; Gideon was afraid; Sampson was a womanizer; Rahab was a prostitute; Jephthah was a bandit, a social and family outcast.

In addition, other people in the Bible not listed in **Hebrews 11** were also failures—Elijah was suicidal; Jonah ran from God; Job went bankrupt; Peter denied Christ three times; Martha worried about everything; Mary Magdalene was demon-possessed and a prostitute; and Paul tortured Christians.

But God used these ordinary people in eternally significant ways when they stepped out in faith. It is truly a joy to know that God does not focus on our failures but on our faith; He wants us to stay under Him and trust Him. He will continue to use us when we exercise faith. He turns our failures into eternal significance through His power.

12. Peace from God replaces anxiety.

We thank God for these negative circumstances and ask God to use them for His best for us for His glory. In response, He promises to provide us peace as we walk through them.

"Be anxious for nothing, but in everything by prayer and supplication, with thanksgiving, let your requests be made known to God; and the peace of God, which surpasses all understanding, will guard your hearts and minds through Christ Jesus" **(Philippians 4:6–7).**

13. God wants to "redirect" us.

Sometimes God allows the difficulty to redirect us for a season. This is what He did with Paul in **Acts 27–28**. He redirected Paul's course.

And He used a winter storm to do it so that Paul was then <u>shipwrecked on Malta</u> so that he could heal, by the power of the Holy Spirit, several people on the island who were sick. And then, after that, God got him back on track to Rome.

The storm didn't come because Paul had done something wrong. It was just the tool that God used for His purposes.

"An umbrella cannot stop the rain, but it allows us to stand in the rain. Faith in God may not remove our trials, but it gives us strength to overcome them." — **The Cool Shady Tree.**

Snoopy would add to that quote and say, *"Life isn't about waiting for the storm to pass. It's about learning to dance in the rain"* (With God).

The simple, concise answer to <u>"Why Me, God?"</u> is that we truly learn that God is good, that He is trustworthy, that He loves us, and He wants the best for us even when bad things happen, that are actually "<u>disguised eternal blessings</u>."

SOME PERSONAL STEPS IN SHOE LEATHER

I, like most children of our Heavenly Father, have had many disappointments in my life where my immediate response was, "Why me, God?"

Some of these include: (1) Having a neck injury in college football that ended my playing career that appeared pro-bound; it also caused me to fail my physical exam to get my second lieutenant commission in the

Army, which ended a potential career in the military. (2) Losing a net worth of several millions of dollars in the real estate business when the US economy crashed, and I was on the verge of declaring bankruptcy. (3) My wife was diagnosed with nonsmoker's lung cancer, which caused her physical death after she suffered tremendously for thirteen years. (4) My oldest grandson was born with ADHD (attention-deficit/hyperactivity disorder) and OCD (obsessive-compulsive disorder).

In looking back on each of these and many other disappointments, I truly see them as "**disguised eternal blessings**." (1) My neck injury allowed me future business opportunities that provided me the necessary time to focus on God's Word and grow in my faith. (2) My loss of millions and almost declaring bankruptcy provided me a worldwide testimony about God's provision that restored my ability to give amounts exceedingly abundantly above anything that I ever imagined. (3) God allowed my wife to lead numerous people to Christ during her cancer journey, including the last two months of her earthly life, where she led her brother to Christ. (4) God trained my grandson in perseverance and diligence, and he just graduated as Salutatorian of his Senior class; was elected President of the Student Body; was awarded his Eagle rank in Boy Scouts; and was the high scorer in his school's basketball team.

I love the saying: *"Be like seeds; do not see dirt thrown at you as your enemy, but as ground on which to grow."*

God continues to show me His immense love. He has taught me most of the preceding thirteen lessons in "Why does He allow bad things to happen to good people?" All that I can really say is, "THANK YOU, GOD!!!"

CHAPTER 11.

GOD'S BEST FOR US

We all desire to have the best in life. From our careers to our love life, we don't want to settle for just good enough or satisfactory. We want the best. **Psalm 37:4** says, *"Delight yourself in the Lord, and He will give you the desires of your heart."* We are all guilty of asking God for our selfish desires, thinking we know what is best for us. In essence, we treat God like Santa Claus, telling Him what we selfishly want.

The Hebrew word for "delight" in this verse means "to be soft and tender." God's children are to be soft and tender toward their Heavenly Father, always teachable, and always pliable in His hands. Our head knowledge accepts **1 John 4:16,** *"We know how much God loves us, and we have put our trust in His love. God is love, and all who live in love live in God, and God lives in them."*

We mentally believe that this loving Father wants the best for His kids. Where we struggle is in God's definition of **BEST,** which appears to have some negative temporal components. **God has each of us in a disciple training program where the "desires of our hearts" become what God in His love defines as "best."**

Jeremiah 33:3 offers the truth that God is a Father who desires to give us clarity and a firm footing of <u>faith</u> in His final Word, "*Call to Me, and I will answer you and tell you great and unsearchable things you do not know.*" We are but humans with limited understanding, knowledge, and insight into what is really happening behind the scenes or what will come later.

How Do We Know, Accept, and Receive God's Best?

God, in His Scripture, provides shoe leather for walking down this path and provides us with some essentials.

(1) <u>Believe God wants the best for us.</u>

God is a good, kind, and loving Father. **Psalm 34:8** says, "*Taste and see that the Lord is good.*" God wants to give us His best. Believe it and expect it. Too often, we think God is mad at us, or we're not worthy of God's best. God's best is not about how good or worthy you are, but it is based on your faith in Jesus and what He did for you.

Jeremiah 29:11 says, "*I know the plans I have for you,*" declares the Lord, "*plans to prosper you and not to harm you, plans to give you hope and a future.*" God has great plans for your life – the best plans. Simply believe God wants the best for you.

(2) <u>Know what God's best is.</u>

Unfortunately, most Christians get focused on their plans and end up missing what God has for them. We spend a lot of effort and time trying to make our plans come to pass. We pray and try to convince God to bless our plans. However, **Proverbs 19:21** tells us, "*There are many plans in a man's heart, but it is the Lord's plan that will stand.*"

The key to knowing God's best is to discover His plan for your life. His plans are already blessed. His plan for you is His best. He will direct your steps and lead you toward His best when you trust Him. **Proverbs 3:5–6** says, "*Trust in the Lord with all your heart, and lean not on your own understanding; in all your ways acknowledge Him, and He shall direct your paths.*" He's not trying to hide it or keep His plan or best from you. Trust Him, and He will direct you in His best.

One of the ways we can discern from God what His best is comes through prayer and revelation given by the Holy Spirit. **John 14** reminds us that the Holy Spirit is the Spirit of Truth, and we can stand firmly on what He says.

We must also be diligent in taking what we hear and believe it to be of God by testing it against God's Word. Does it align with Scripture, and do you have a peace that can only come from God from such a Word? These are questions we must ask along the way.

Finally, we must step aside from what we want the answer to be to hear clearly what His answer truly is. This looks like laying your own hopeful answer at His feet to receive the answer truly and fully He has for you, even if that answer is not to your temporal desire.

"*Disappointments are just God's way of saying – I've got something better. So be patient; have faith; and live your life.*" — **Anonymous**

(3)   God's best many times involves trials, discipline, and suffering.

James 1:2–4 instructs us, "*Consider it pure joy, my brothers and sisters, whenever you face trials of many kinds, because you know that the testing of your faith produces perseverance. Let perseverance finish its work so that you may be mature and complete, not lacking anything.*"

Hebrews 12:10 says, "*He disciplines us for our good, that we may share in His holiness*"—the ultimate essential of character.

Trials and discipline provide suffering that teaches us that God's best in the Christian life is not the absence of pain. **God's best in the Christian life is transforming us into Christlikeness.** "*For just as the sufferings of Christ are ours in abundance, so also our comfort is abundant through Christ*" **(2 Corinthians 1:5).**

Suffering teaches us that God is more concerned about character than He is about comfort. "*Not only that, but we rejoice in our sufferings, knowing that suffering produces endurance, and endurance produces character, and character produces hope, and hope does not put us to shame, because God's love has been poured into our hearts through the Holy Spirit who has been given to us*" **(Romans 5:3–5).**

Suffering bankrupts our resources and therefore makes us dependent upon God. "*But He (God) said,' My grace is sufficient for you, for my power is made perfect in weakness.' Therefore, I will boast all the more gladly of my weaknesses so that the power of Christ may rest upon me*" **(2 Corinthians 12:9).**

Suffering also teaches us humility (the opposite of pride). Paul realizes that truth and expresses it in **2 Corinthians 12:7**. *"The things God showed me were so great. But to keep me from being too full of pride because of seeing these things, I have been given trouble in my body. It was sent from Satan to hurt me. It keeps me from being proud."*

Suffering enables us to help others in their trials. *"God comforts us in all our troubles so that we can comfort those in any trouble with the comfort we ourselves receive from God"* **(2 Corinthians 1:4)**.

Suffering produces a broken and contrite heart, which delights God, according to **Psalm 51:17.** Suffering reveals what and who we really love. Suffering is a test of our love.

Trials teach us to value the favor of God because, in the midst of trials, that's the only thing that we cry out for, the loving-kindness of God. *"Because Your lovingkindness is better than life, my lips shall praise You"* **(Psalm 63:3)**. When life gets down to the bare level of existence in the midst of anguish, the loving-kindness of God becomes enough.

James 1:2–4 teaches us that trials produce a mature and complete faith in which we believe and trust God in every step of our life journey.

"God always gives you all the grace you need. So, you will only have to suffer for a little while. Then God Himself will build you up again. He will make you strong and steady. And He has chosen you to share in His eternal glory because you belong to Christ" **(1 Peter 5:10)**.

(4) God's best has an eternal perspective.

The Christian life is all about an eternal perspective. Whatever happens or doesn't happen in our short temporal earthly life is not the objective and the goal. *"For our light affliction, which is but for a moment, worketh for us a far more exceeding and eternal weight of glory, while we look not at the things which are seen, but at the things which are not seen. For the things which are seen are temporal, but the things which are not seen are eternal."* **(2 Corinthians 4:17–18)**

Colossians 3:1–3 *says, "Since then you have been raised with Christ, set your hearts on things above, where Christ is, seated at the right hand of God. Set your mind on the things above, not on earthly things. For you died, and your life is now hidden with Christ in God."*

(5) Wait for God's timing on His best.

Most of us hate waiting. We want what we want when we want it. However, impatience is seldom the recipe for God's best. Instead, it tends to get us into trouble. It is through faith and patience that we obtain the promises of God **(Hebrews 6:12)**. Often, because of our lack of patience, we end up settling for less than God's best.

Even Abraham and Sarah became impatient with God. God had promised them a son, but when it didn't happen as quickly as they wanted, they short-circuited God's plan and conceived Ishmael. Ishmael was good; he just wasn't God's best, and it created problems for Abraham and the whole world.

Over and over, the Israelites also decided to run ahead of God's best for them. They grew weary of waiting for God to fulfill His promises. They wondered if God had their best in mind or if He could be trusted at all. But Isaiah offered them hope:

"Since ancient times, no one has heard, no ear has perceived, no eye has seen any God besides you, who acts on behalf of those who wait for him" (**Isaiah 64:4**).

Isaiah wanted to elevate the Israelites' view of God so they would learn to trust Him more. No other god can do what God can do. No one can perceive, hear, or see God's plan until He reveals it. Only He knows what is best because no one else compares to Him.

When we understand God is good, we can trust He has good in store for us. When we know Him as the sovereign Lord over our prayers, plans, and hopes, we can believe He wants our best. When we wait for God to act on our behalf, we receive the fullness of His blessings.

Maybe you are struggling to wait for God's best. Everything in your heart, mind, or flesh may be crying out for a shortcut—one that will relieve the pressures of life *right now*.

When we're tempted to run ahead of God's best, He's never further away than a quick prayer. *"Help me. Save me. Comfort me."* God loves to hear our short, sweet prayers of trust. As we lean on God instead of our own desires, He'll act on our behalf.

Though we can't hear, perceive, or see God's master plan for our life, we can trust Him today in our struggles. Surrender all our hopes and desires to Him. Keep praying for as long as it takes. His presence will be an incomparable comfort if we choose to wait. *"Let us not become weary in doing good, for at the proper time we will reap a harvest if we do not give up"* (**Galatians 6:9**).

(6) Thank and Praise God for His best.

"In everything give thanks; for this is the will of the Father concerning you through Christ Jesus" (**1 Thessalonians 5:18**). Keep a heart of thanksgiving even in the darkest times when trials and suffering surround us.

When things are going well – praise Him! Praise helps take the focus off us and put it back on God. It is all about God, not us. Praise helps keep us in a place of humility. As we praise Him, we recognize we are totally dependent upon Him – it is all about Him – not us. Praise opens the gateway of God's blessing and His best as we come into the Presence of our King.

"Enter His gates with thanksgiving and His courts with praise! Give thanks to Him; bless His name!" (**Psalms 100:4**).

(7) God's very best is Jesus.

God's very best is Jesus, who came into this world to show you God's grace. Jesus, who suffered so terribly to take the punishment that you and I so richly deserve so that we can have a real, intimate, powerful, and eternity-long relationship with God.

That's the whole purpose of everything Jesus did for you and for me—to open the door to that tender, intimate relationship with Him. God's cry from the beginning of the Bible to the end is His desire to be our God and for us to be His people. He wants to dwell in our midst and for us to be with Him and behold His glory and enjoy His presence and worship Him in a way that is completely divine.

In **Revelation 21:1–7,** God repeats His cry, a cry that we hear repeatedly through Scripture, but this time it is the fulfillment of His deepest desire; it is a glimpse into our future.

"Then I saw a new heaven and a new earth for the first heaven, and the first earth had passed away, and the sea was no more, and I saw the Holy city, the new Jerusalem coming down out of heaven from God prepared as a bride adorned for her husband and I heard a loud voice saying from the throne, 'see the home of God is among mortals.

He will dwell with them; they will be His people, and God himself will be with them; he will wipe away every tear from their eyes; death will be no more, mourning and crying and pain will be no more for the first things have passed away. And the one who was seated on the throne said, 'See, I am making all things new.' Also, he said, 'Write this for these words are trustworthy and true.'

Then he said to me, 'It is done; I am the alpha and the omega, the beginning and the end. To the thirsty, I will give water as a gift from the spring of the water of life. Those who conquer will inherit these things, and I will be their God, and they will be my children."

That's God's very best for you, eternity with Him through Jesus, His Son, and that's not something that begins when you die; it's something that begins the moment you believe in Jesus and accept Him as your savior.

God's wisdom knows what's best for you, and His love wants what's best for you, and God's power ensures you receive what's best for you. We can know something is God's best for us when we stop assuming and trying to journey through life only occasionally involving God.

Instead, we must ask God what He wants us to know. This requires humility, the dying of self, and the thought that, somehow, we know better than God Himself. **Luke 9:23** reminds us, *"And he said to all, "If anyone would come after me, let him deny himself and take up his cross daily and follow me."*

It is a daily practice to die to the idea that we somehow know what is best for us because we really do not. Thankfully, we have a Father who does know what is best for us, and when we follow Him and His leading, we find ourselves in a place where we can receive God's best.

"God knows what His best is for you, and you are worthy of His best. So do not settle for what is good enough right now in the present when just around the corner, He could have something far greater than you could possibly ever ask for or imagine." — **Cally Logan**, American author and teacher

---

SOME PERSONAL STEPS IN SHOE LEATHER

One of the most effective Christian leaders in the world is currently struggling with the evident reality that his 80+ years old wife, who is in hospice, will soon be going home to God. He is holding on to a dream that his wife had several years ago that she would live past 100 years of age and leave for Heaven after he had already gone.

When told of this, I shared with his son my journey on a similar path. My wife had nonsmoking lung cancer for thirteen years and had several surgeries, chemotherapy, and radiation treatments. We had literally hundreds praying for her physical healing for years. In the last year of her earthly life, she was begging God to bring her Home to Heaven. She was truly suffering from the pain, and her physical body was wasting away.

In the last two months, I started praying and asking others to pray for God's best for her. God is our Heavenly Father who loves us more than we are capable of loving, and He truly does want the best for His kids. In those two months, God allowed my wife to lead her brother to salvation in Christ over the telephone. She had been trying for years to encourage him to accept Christ as his savior. Her brother died a few weeks after my wife, but because of God's grace, he headed to Heaven to join his sister.

She also led a mother struggling with alcohol to Christ. In addition, she handed out cards with the verse in **John 3:16** printed on them to all her hospice caregivers, *"For God so loved the world that He gave His only begotten Son so that whoever believes in Him shall not perish but have eternal life."*

I encouraged the Christian leader's son to ask his anguishing dad to pray for God's best which brought me contentment and peace and obviously resulted in outcomes that were eternally significant.

CHAPTER 12.
HOLES IN OUR SHOE LEATHER

As was mentioned in the Introduction, the strongest and toughest shoe leather is that provided by our loving Heavenly Father—His Word. God's shoe leather doesn't remove the obstacles in our journey but provides peace, joy, and comfort as we walk through them.

As we journey through life, particularly through the rocky and difficult terrain of problems, consequences of poor choices, trials, etc., that promote pain and suffering, we begin to develop holes in our shoe leather. We no longer focus on God's Word to provide support but instead focus on the obstacles. The longer that we allow an obstacle to constrain our journey with God, the bigger the hole because of not trusting God in His Word.

We will consider what appear to be seven of the most major obstacles which can cause holes in our shoe leather during our life journey: sin, doubt, fear, unforgiveness, hate, laziness, and greed.

(1) SIN

The word "sin" as it appears in the Bible comes from the Greek word "Hamartia" in the New Testament and the Hebrew word "Hata" in the Old Testament, which both mean "to miss the mark" or "flawed." The word was used in archery and spear-throwing when a person missed the center of the target.

Sin becomes a failure or missing the mark to become believers who fully love God and others. We look at sin in a vertical way where murder is on the top and something like a "white lie "is on the bottom. However, God looks at sin in a horizontal way where all sin (no matter how big or small in our eyes) separates us from God. Observing the cross of Christ, God wants to tell us that Christ's sacrifice covers all sin no matter how it is viewed, both in the vertical as well as in the horizontal.

Adrian Rogers warns, "*Don't let a little sin in; all hell will break loose. Sin is not just breaking God's laws; it is breaking His heart.*"

Here is the danger for you and for me: sin doesn't always look sinful to us. It's hard to admit it, but all too often, sin looks beautiful to us, and we fall into the trap, not realizing at the moment that what we are about to do is sin. Part of the deceptive power of sin in my heart is the ability for it to look beautiful when it is terribly ugly. This is certainly displayed in the first sin recorded in **Genesis 3:6,** "*So, when the woman saw that the tree was good for food and that it was a delight to the eyes, and that the tree was to be desired to make one wise, she took of its fruit and ate, and she also gave some to her husband who was with her, and he ate.*"

This first sin had all three basic elements described in **1 John 2:16** *"For everything in the world—the lust of the flesh, the lust of the eyes, and the pride of life—comes not from the Father but from the world."* Most, if not all, of our sins can be categorized under one of these three elements. C.S. Lewis feels that pride is the main culprit, *"Pride has been the chief cause of misery in every nation and every family since the world began."*

The eternal "Good News" is stated in **1 Corinthians 15:56–57**, *"The sting of death is sin, and the power of sin is the Law; but thanks be to God, who gives us the victory through our Lord Jesus Christ."* In reality, the eternal war against sin has been won; Jesus Christ has saved all who trust in Him and His victory.

However, we still have ongoing earthly battles. We need to fight these constant battles against sin that invade us from all directions. In our earthly battles against sin, we are called to wrestle, run, fight, and pray.

We, believers, have been washed clean by the blood of Jesus shed on the cross, but we still sin and need continuous confession (agreeing with God about our sins). In **1 John 1:9,** we believers are instructed, *"If we confess our sins, he is faithful and just to forgive us our sins and to cleanse us from all unrighteousness."* This is Jesus' foot washing verse whereby our feet get dirty with sin in this world even though we have been washed eternally clean. Unconfessed sin will cause a hole in our shoe leather, causing unnecessary pain and consequences.

God has provided an offensive weapon for each of us to fight these ongoing battles against sin, revealed in **Ephesians 6:17,** *"...the sword* *of the Spirit, which is the Word of God"* All who are willing to embrace the truths of God's Word will enjoy more and more freedom from sin. *"If you continue in my word then you are my disciples indeed, and you will know the truth, and the truth will set you free"* **(John 8:31–32).** The Word of God provides the necessary solid shoe leather on which to journey through life.

A more comforting truth exists in our war against sin. *"But you have received the Holy Spirit, and He lives within you, in your hearts, so that you don't need anyone to teach you what is right. For He teaches you all things, and He is the Truth and no liar; and so, just as He has said, you must live in Christ, never to depart from Him"* **(1 John 2:27).** Our ever-present traveling companion, as was discussed in Chapter 5, will be our ready warrior in our daily fight and guard against sin. *"He wants to be our Helper, and it grieves Him when we walk in sin"* **(Ephesians 4:30).**

(2) DOUBT

Doubt is defined as "a feeling of uncertainty or lack of conviction." Webster's dictionary defines doubt as *"to call into question the truth of or to be uncertain."* Doubt is an experience common to all people.

Even those with faith in God struggle with doubt on occasion and say with the man in **Mark 9:24**, *"I do believe; help me overcome my unbelief."* Some people are hindered greatly by doubt; some see it as a springboard to life, and others see it as an obstacle to overcome. Doubt is not from God. Doubt comes from the evil one who seeks to destroy our intimate relationships with God. Place your faith in your Heavenly Father, and know you are protected.

Howard Hendricks at Dallas Theological Seminary taught, *"We should never doubt in the dark what we learned in the light."*

God in His Word provides examples of people who struggled with doubt. God spoke and shared the news of a child with Abraham. Abraham knew God, and yet he still doubted. *"Abraham fell facedown; he laughed and said to himself, Will a son be born to a man a hundred years old? Will Sarah bear a child at the age of ninety?"* (**Genesis 17:17**)

Thomas, one of the disciples of Jesus, doubted. When the other disciples told Thomas that they had seen the resurrected Lord, he didn't believe them. He wanted tangible proof. *"So, the other disciples told him, 'We have seen the Lord!' But he said to them, 'Unless I see the nail marks in his hands and put my finger where the nails were, and put my hand into his side, I will not believe.'"* (**John 20:25**)

How often have you wanted something before you believed? Even though Thomas was part of the inner circle of Jesus, he would not believe until his demand was answered. Did that make Jesus love Thomas any less? No. Jesus knew there would be doubters. Jesus knew to worry, and concern was shared by many. Jesús chose to give Thomas the answer he wanted. *"A week later, His disciples were in the house again, and Thomas was with them. Though the doors were locked, Jesus came and stood among them and said, 'Peace be with you!' Then he said to Thomas, 'Put your finger here; see my hands. Reach out your hand and put it into my side. Stop doubting and believe.'"* (***John 20:26–27***) The next words of Jesus are impactful to us all. *"Then Jesus told him, 'Because you have seen me, you have believed; blessed are those who have not seen and yet have believed'"* (**John 20:29**).

Although we have not physically seen Jesus, we can believe and know Him. The Bible is the Word of God. Doubt will come. The way we deal with that doubt will either deepen our relationship with our Heavenly Father or pull us away from Him.

Faith is believing and trusting in God, knowing that He loves us and wants the best for us. As born-again Christians, we have the opportunity to rest in our faith in God. When doubt comes, we can immediately go to God in prayer and ask for guidance. Resting in Him allows our faith to grow stronger.

"But those who hope in the Lord will renew their strength. They will soar on wings like eagles; they will run and not grow weary; they will walk and not be faint" **(Isaiah 40:31).** *As* soon as we release our doubt to Him, our faith will strengthen and prevail against uncertainty.

Adrian Rogers concludes, *"Pray and doubt; you'll do without. Pray and believe; you will receive."*

(3) FEAR

"Fear defeats more people than any other thing in the world." — **Ralph Waldo Emerson.**

As we each know in our life journey, fear is something that is entangled in every aspect of our lives. According to statistical studies, more than 30% of adults in the United States struggle with anxiety disorders or phobias. Our fears can cause us to trust in things, people, places, idols, etc., instead of trusting in God, who created and breathed life into us.

The term "fear not," or similar verbiage, is stated in the Bible 365 times. Some recognized Scripture verses include **Psalm 34:4,** *"I sought the Lord, and he answered me and delivered me from all my fears,"* and **2 Timothy 1:7,** *"For God has not given us a spirit of fear, but of power and of love and of a sound mind."*

According to the most-downloaded Bible app YouVersion, installed on over 500 million devices, the most shared Bible verse of 2022 is the same as in 2020 during the rise of COVID. It also occupied the top spot in 2018. *"Fear not, for I am with you; do not be afraid, for I am your God. I will strengthen you; I will also help you; I will also uphold you with My righteous right hand"* **(Isaiah 41:10).**

Through Jesus's sacrifice and resurrection, people have a Savior who took the punishment for our sins and brought us to a place where God only wants to offer love, peace, and the opportunity to serve alongside Him.

Fear can be crippling and push the most composed people into states of utter discomfort and uncertainty, but God reminds people through His Word that because of Jesus, there is nothing to fear. Even with death or failure, which are prevalent fears among born-again Christians (as well as of non-Christians) who believe in heaven and know that God loves them despite mistakes they make, Jesus can still remove those fears.

The best definition that I have ever heard for **FEAR is "allowing someone or something to control you."** We, born-again Christians, need to fear God and Him alone. Let Him control us by His indwelling Holy Spirit with His love and His best for us. *"Have I not commanded you? Be strong and courageous. Do not be afraid; do not be discouraged, for the LORD your*

God will be with you wherever you go" (**Joshua 1:9**). *"The fear of the Lord is the beginning of wisdom, And the knowledge of the Holy One is understanding"* (**Proverbs 9:10**). *"The fear of the Lord is a fountain of life, that one may avoid the snares of death"* (**Proverbs 14:27**). *"Keep your lives free from the love of money and be content with what you have, because God has said, 'Never will I leave you; never will I forsake you.' So, we say with confidence, The Lord is my helper; I will not be afraid. What can mere mortals do to me?"* (**Hebrews 13:5–6**).

(4)   UNFORGIVENESS

We're all guilty of offending other people, and we've all been offended by other people; that's the fact of living in a sinful world. But as Christians, we're told to be forgiving people. It's impossible to live a victorious Christian life with unforgiveness in our life. It isn't the offense that destroys relationships; it's the inability to forgive that destroys relationships.

Unforgiveness is a sin that locks the unforgiving person in their own self-made prison. It's as bad as being enslaved to mind-altering drugs or alcoholism. Unforgiveness is a sin that will destroy its own container. Unforgiveness is a sin that will destroy you like an incurable cancer. People often say: "I don't get mad; I get even." People mistakenly believe that their bitterness and refusal to forgive will make the other person suffer. But it's the unforgiving person that suffers! **Unforgiveness is the poison that you drink, hoping the other person dies.**

Jesus said in **Mark 11:25–26**, *"Whenever you stand praying if you have anything against anyone, forgive him, that your Father in heaven may also forgive you your trespasses. But if you do not forgive, neither will your Father* *in heaven forgive your trespasses."* This isn't about our eternal salvation; that's secure when we put our faith in Jesus Christ as our Lord and Savior. This is about our being blessed or disciplined by God (**Hebrews 12:7–11**).

Unforgiveness is usually a result of ungodly pride and self-righteousness. Unforgiveness is often the sin that's committed against those with whom we are the closest and dearest. There are the sayings "Familiarity breeds contempt." and "Why do we always hurt the ones we love?" Unforgiveness is often a family sin. Husbands won't forgive their wives; wives won't forgive their husbands; children won't forgive their parents, and parents won't forgive their children. Unforgiveness among fellow believers is, sadly, common.

Neil T. Anderson, in his book, "The Bondage Breaker," said, *"Forgiveness is agreeing to live with the consequences of another person's sin. Forgiveness is costly; we pay the price of the evil we forgive. Yet you're going to live with those consequences whether you want to or not; your only choice is whether you will live in the bitterness of unforgiveness or the freedom of forgiveness. That's how Jesus forgave you—He took the consequences of your sin upon Himself. All true forgiveness is substitutional because no one really forgives without bearing the penalty of the other person's sin."* Forgiveness is extending mercy to those who have harmed us.

Living a lifestyle of forgiveness is commanded for Christians. *"Forgive as the Lord forgave you"* (**Colossians 3:13**). *"Let all bitterness, wrath, anger, clamor, and evil speaking be put away from you, with all malice. And be kind to one another, tenderhearted, forgiving one another, even as God in Christ forgave you"* (**Ephesians 4:31–32**).

(5) HATE

The Bible informs us that there are positive and negative aspects to "hate." It is acceptable to hate those things that God hates; indeed, this is very much proof of a loving relationship with God. *"Let those who love the Lord hate evil"* (**Psalm 97:10**). Indeed, the closer our walk with the Lord and the more we fellowship with Him, the more conscious we will be of sin, both within and without.

However, the hatred that is negative is that which is directed against others. **Martin Luther King, Jr.** proclaimed, *"Like unchecked cancer, hate corrodes the personality and eats away its vital unity. Hate destroys a man's sense of values and his objectivity. It causes him to describe the beautiful as ugly and the ugly as beautiful, and to confuse the true with the false and the false with the true."*

The Lord mentions hatred in the Sermon on the Mount. In **Matthew 5:22**, we read *"But I tell you that anyone who is angry with his brother will be subject to judgment."* The Lord commands that not only should we be reconciled with our brother before we go before the Lord, but also that we do it quickly (**Matthew 5:23–26**).

The act of murder itself was certainly condemned, but hate is a "heart" sin, and any hateful thought or act is an act of murder in God's eyes. So heinous is the position of hate before God that a man who hates is said to be walking in darkness, as opposed to the light (**1 John 2:9, 11**). As with all sins of born-again Christians, Jesus Christ paid for them completely on the cross. However, our loving Heavenly Father will provide discipline and further earthly instruction and teaching for His children struggling with sin, including hate.

God directs His children in **Romans 12:17–21,** *"Do not repay anyone evil for evil. Be careful to do what is right in the eyes of everyone. If it is possible, as far as it depends on you, live at peace with everyone. Do not take revenge, my dear friends, but leave room for God's wrath, for it is written: 'It is mine to avenge; I will repay,' says the Lord. On the contrary, 'If your enemy is hungry, feed him; if he is thirsty, give him something to drink. In doing this, you will heap burning coals on his head.' Do not be overcome by evil but overcome evil with good."*

Martin Luther King, Jr. states this underlying truth, *"Darkness cannot drive out darkness; only light can do that. Hate cannot drive out hate; only love can do that."*

(6) LAZINESS

Ancient Greek **Sophocles** stated, *"Laziness is the mother of all evils."*

The Bible has much to say about laziness, as well as its opposite, diligent work. The topic of laziness, although found throughout the Bible, is most often referred to in the Old Testament book of Proverbs. The words most often used to describe laziness are "sluggard" and "slothful." These terms are more illustrative than the term "lazy,"

When I lived in Venezuela, I saw this animal, a sloth, which I had never seen before, and I was amazed that it's every movement was so slow. In fact, a sloth moves on the ground at a lazy six and a half feet per minute. Similarly, a certain type of slug clocks in at an astoundingly slow pace of six and a half inches in two hours.

The word "sluggard" appears fourteen times in the book of Proverbs. The sluggard or lazy person is characterized by excessive sleep (**Proverbs 6:9–11; 26:14**), excuse-making (**Proverbs 22:13**), and conceit (**Proverbs 26:16**). Proverbs also tells us the end in store for the lazy: A lazy person becomes a servant (or debtor): "*Diligent hands will rule, but laziness ends in slave labor*" (**Proverbs 12:24**); his future is bleak: "*A sluggard does not plow in season; so at harvest time he looks but finds nothing*" (**Proverbs 20:4**); he may come to poverty: "*The soul of the lazy man desires and has nothing, but the soul of the diligent shall be made rich*" (**Proverbs 13:4**). Laziness is clearly not the way of the wise. Laziness, a lifestyle for some, is a temptation for all.

God created mankind to work (**Genesis 2:15**). Laziness, being a sin, has disastrous consequences, as do all sins (**Romans 6:23**). In fact, Scripture states that those who are able to work, but refuse to do so, should not be allowed to eat (**2 Thessalonians 3:10–12**). Those who work but in a lazy manner are an irritation to their employers, as smoke is an irritant to the eyes (**Proverbs 10:26**). Rather than being lazy, we diligently work and rest as God has called us.

There is no room for laziness in the life of a Christian. A new believer is truthfully taught in **Ephesians 2:8–9**, "*...it is by grace you have been saved, through faith—and this not from yourselves, it is the gift of God—not by works, so that no one can boast.*" But a believer can become idle if he erroneously believes God expects no fruit from a transformed life. "*For we are God's workmanship, created in Christ Jesus to do good works, which God prepared in advance for us to do*" (**Ephesians 2:10**).

Christians are not saved by works, but they do show their faith by their works (**James 2:18, 26**). Slothfulness violates God's purpose—good works.

We also remember in **Philippians 2:13,** *"It is God who works in you, both to will and to work for his good pleasure,"* and He is faithful to complete the good work He began in us (**Philippians 1:6**).

Christians are not called to be man-pleasers but God-pleasers. Christians are called to serve the Lord with zeal in whatever we do (**Romans 12:11; 1 Corinthians 10:31; Colossians 3:17**). This is why all occupations (except sinful ones) can be performed as acts of worship and service to Christ.

It is not merely the external act that makes work acceptable to God but the internal disposition of the heart. One person may preach for selfish gain and therefore displease God. Another person may sweep floors for Jesus and thereby glorify God. Working at the tasks that God has entrusted to us with a heart of worship rather than a disposition of laziness glorifies God.

When it comes to laziness, we do well to recall the exhortation of **Romans 12:11** *"Do not be slothful in zeal, be fervent in spirit, serve the Lord."* **This certainly also applies to older believers who may "retire" from secular work but are encouraged to "refire" in their service to the Lord.** *"Therefore, my beloved brothers and sisters, be firm, immovable, always excelling in the work of the Lord, knowing that your labor is not in vain in the Lord"* (**1 Corinthians 15:58**).

(7) GREED

A greedy person is someone whose primary goal in life is to get more and more of something they want, and their whole focus is on getting it. We usually think of money when we think of greed, but a person can be greedy for other things also—food, fame, possessions, prestige, and so forth.

The primary problem is that a greedy person allows things to take the place of God in his/her life. Instead of putting God and His will first, a greedy person puts money and things first. Greed is also wrong because a greedy person is concerned only with himself and overlooks the needs of others. Greed can also lead to other sins, such as jealousy and envy.

The Bible repeatedly warns us against greed, and we need to take its warnings very seriously—especially in our materialistic society. Jesus said in **Luke 12:15**, *"Watch out! Be on your guard against all kinds of greed; a man's life does not consist in the abundance of his possessions."* **Proverbs 28:25** also says, *"A greedy man stirs up dissension, but he who trusts in the Lord will prosper."*

Greed is a serious sin to be avoided; however, the Bible views wealth as a serious responsibility to do good. All wealth comes from God as a gift entrusted to us to use properly for Him. We are free to enjoy without guilt the wealth God bestows, but we're also stewards of it for Him. Paul's counsel applies to us in **1 Timothy 6:17–18,** *"Instruct those who are rich in this present world not to be conceited or to fix their hope on the uncertainty of riches, but on God, who richly supplies us with all things to enjoy. Instruct them to do good, to be rich in good works, to be generous and ready to share."*

"One gains by losing self for others and not by hoarding for oneself." — **Watchman Nee**, Chinese Christian teacher and leader

Fostering a giving and generous heart will drive greed out of our hearts by the power of the love of God. **Generosity is the cure for greed.**

In conclusion, born-again Christians are on a journey through life with God. When on this earth, which is full of obstacles, we must have a thick layer of shoe leather (the Word of God) with no holes to allow us the confidence, peace, and joy of an abundant journey.

SOME PERSONAL STEPS IN SHOE LEATHER

I wish I could say these seven obstacles appeared horribly ugly and destructive to me, but I can't. I wish I could say that I always hate what God hates, but I can't. I wish I could say that I always love to do what is right, but I can't. I wish I could never say that my way is better than God's. But I can't. I wish I could say that my battles with sin and these obstacles are over, but I can't. Praise God for His Word to provide us with shoe leather for our life journeys and realize He walks with us to avoid these potential "holes."

EPILOGUE

ROMAN ROAD TO SALVATION

In our shoe leather life journey with God, we have traveled down many pathways and roads. **If a person has not traveled down the Roman Road in his/her life yet, it is the most important road with which to start because it leads to salvation.** This road has a collection of verses from the book of Romans explaining God's free gift of eternal life. Follow these verses to learn why we need salvation, God's plan of salvation, how to receive salvation, God's promise of eternal life, and the results of salvation.

1st stop on the Roman Road to Salvation...

God Is the Creator of Life

"For since the creation of the world God's invisible qualities – His eternal power and divine nature – have been clearly seen, being understood from what has been made, so that men are without excuse. For although they knew God, they neither glorified Him as God nor gave thanks to Him, but their thinking became futile, and their foolish hearts were darkened" **(Romans 1:20–21).** God reveals Himself to us—His divine nature and personal

qualities—through creation. We must acknowledge God as the Creator and Sustainer of life.

2nd stop on the Roman Road to Salvation...

Why We Need Salvation – The Fact of Our Sin

"For all have sinned and fall short of the glory of God" **(Romans 3:23).** We must recognize that we are sinners and that we do not meet God's perfect standards. Sin is serious in God's sight and includes thoughts, words, and actions. All sin (i.e., hatred and lust) makes us sinners, not just the big, obvious sins like murder and adultery **(Romans 5:12).**

3rd stop on the Roman Road to Salvation...

Man's Inability

"As it is written: There is no one righteous, not even one" **(Romans 3:10).** No one can earn right standing with God. We must understand that our good deeds or religion are unacceptable to God because our good works cannot cancel out our sin. For a view of man's sinful condition, read **Romans 3:10–18.**

4th stop on the Roman Road to Salvation...

The Penalty of Sin

"For the wages of sin is death" **(Romans 6:23a).** God's holiness demands a penalty (consequence) for our sin, which is death. Eternal death is

separation from God forever in Hell. God is a just God, and He demands punishment for every sin. Justice is getting what we deserve, because of our sin, we deserve death.

5th stop on the Roman Road to Salvation...

God's Plan of Salvation

"But God demonstrates His own love for us in this: While we were still sinners, Christ died for us" (**Romans 5:8**). God sent His Son Jesus Christ to pay the penalty for our sin by dying on the cross. God is a God of mercy and He sent Jesus to take our sin upon Himself and the punishment we deserve. Mercy is not getting what we deserve, we deserve death, and Jesus took our place.

6th stop on the Roman Road to Salvation...

God's Promise of Eternal Life

"For the wages of sin is death, but the gift of God is eternal life in Christ Jesus our Lord" (**Romans 6:23**). Eternal life is a free gift from God, there is nothing we can do to earn eternal life. Grace is getting what we don't deserve. Because of God's amazing grace, He has given us eternal life through Jesus Christ!

7th stop on the Roman Road to Salvation...

Man's Responsibility

"That if you confess with your mouth, 'Jesus is Lord,' and believe in your heart that God raised Him from the dead, you will be saved. For it is with your heart that you believe and are justified, and it is with your mouth that you confess and are saved" **(Romans 10:9–10).** We must believe that the Lord Jesus Christ is the Son of God who died for us on the cross, rose from the dead, and is Lord. We must put our trust in Jesus alone to make us right with God. Salvation involves believing in our hearts (inward belief) and an outward confession that Jesus is Lord.

"For everyone who calls on the name of the Lord will be saved" **(Romans 10:13).** There is no complicated formula to salvation; Jesus paid the price of our sin for us. Our response is to accept Jesus as our Lord and Savior. If we do, we will be saved from eternal death in Hell to eternal life in Heaven.

Final Stop on the Roman Road to Salvation...

Results Of Salvation

"Therefore, there is now no condemnation for those who are in Christ Jesus" **(Romans 8:1).** By accepting Jesus' death as a payment for our sins, we will never be condemned for our sins.

"Therefore, since we have been justified through faith, we have peace with God through our Lord Jesus Christ" **(Romans 5:1).** Peace with God means we have been reconciled to Him through Jesus Christ. We can now have a relationship with the living God because sin no longer separates us from Him.

Are you uncertain that if you were to die today you would go to Heaven?

Have you followed the Roman Road to salvation?

Will you accept Jesus Christ as your Lord and Savior today?

You can **pray to God right now** and claim the promises of His Word as your own.

- **Admit that you have sinned against God and ask Him for forgiveness.**

- **Believe that the Lord Jesus Christ is the Son of God who died for you on the cross, rose from the dead, and is Lord.**

- **Call upon Jesus Christ to be your Lord and Savior.**

If you have accepted Jesus as your Lord and Savior today or in the past, we praise God for your decision. You are now on a personal life journey with your Heavenly Father!

This book, "Shoe Leather For Our Life Journey" is not intended to replace the Bible but only to provide some helpful commentary for various parts of your journey. You need to make a steady daily diet of God's Word by getting involved in a Bible study group in a Bible believing and teaching church and by personally reading and studying God's Word.

God's Holy Spirit will help to teach you along your journey.

BIBLIOGRAPHY

Periodicals and Articles

All the glory goes to God, who has enlightened His adopted children with truth and practical shoe leather in all areas of this book. God has given me the spiritual gift of teaching, which He has provided me the privilege of using for decades. He also has provided His wisdom and knowledge to those who have written these articles and periodicals to bring Him glory.

American Medical Association. (1986, March). *The Physical Death of Jesus Christ.*

Bailey, M. (n.d.). *21 Bible Verses on Trial and Tribulation. Beliefnet.com.*

Bright, B. (n.d.). *The Spirit Filled Life. Campus Crusade for Christ (CRU).*

Cole, S. J. (2014, December 14). *Lesson 76: Doing Greater Works Than Jesus (John 14:12-14).*

Cole, S. J. (2016). *When Greed Becomes God. Bible.org.*

Compelling Truth. (n.d.). *Laziness - What Does the Bible Say? Compellingtruth.org.*

Deibert, B. (2022, August 8). *What Are the Gifts of the Holy Spirit? Scripture Quotes and Meaning. Christianity.com.*

Díaz-Pabón, L. Á. (2023, January 6). *Who Is the Holy Spirit? – 5 Things You Need to Know*. Biblestudytools.com.

Dolores Smyth. (2020, February 28). *What Is the Meaning of the Lord's Prayer?* Crosswalk.com.

Edwards, B. (2018, June 22). *How to receive God's best – 4 simple keys for God's best*. Breakthroughforyou.com.

Ganz, R. L. (2021, March 4). *6 Ways to Take Your Thoughts Captive as 2 Corinthians 10:5 Says*. Crosswalk.com.

Geringer, S. (2020, June 26). *Waiting for God's Best*. Proverbs 31 Ministries.

Graham, B. (2007, September 24). *What is Your Definition of a Greedy Person?*

Got Questions Ministries. (n.d.). *Does God Have a Plan for Me?* Gotquestions.org.

Got Questions Ministries. (n.d.). *What does John 14:12 mean?* Bibleref.com.

Got Questions Ministries. (n.d.). *What does the Bible teach about the Trinity?* Bibleref.com.

Got Questions Ministries. (n.d.). *What does the Bible say about doubt?* Gotquestions.org.

Got Questions Ministries. (n.d.). What does the Bible say about hate? Gotquestions.org.

Got Questions Ministries. (n.d.). What does the Bible say about laziness? Gotquestions.org.

Got Questions Ministries. (n.d.). Why does God allow bad things to happen to good people? Gotquestions.org.

Got Questions. (n.d.). What Does the Bible say About Doubt? Gotquestions.org.

Herring, H. (n.d.). 7 Keys to Experiencing God's Best. HaroldHerring.com.

Haynes Jr., C. L. (2020, July 6). 3 Reasons Proverbs 23:7 Says 'As a Man Thinks, So He Is. Crosswalk.com.

Henderson, M. (2022, July 18). What Does the Bible Say About Doubt. Christianity.com.

Historicity of Jesus. (n.d.). In Wikipedia. Retrieved June 9, 2023, from <u>https://en.wikipedia.org/wiki/Historicity_of_Jesus</u>

Lawrence, C. (2021, February 23). The Self-Destructive Sin of Unforgiveness. Agairupdate.com.

Live A Victorious Christian Life. (n.d.). 13 Reasons Why God Allows Trials in Our Lives. Christianlivingtips.com.

Logan, C. (2023, January 10). *How Do We Know What God's Best for Us Is?* Crosswalk.com.

MacArthur, J. (n.d.). *An Eternal Perspective on Temporal Trials.* Grace To You.

McDowell, J. (n.d.). *Is there really solid evidence for the resurrection of Jesus?* Josh McDowell Ministry (CRU).

Noyes, P. (2022, October 5). *10 Roles of the Holy Spirit in the Life of Christians.* Christianity.com.

Oliver, E. (n.d.). *How the Bible Defines Sin and Why It Matters.* Justdisciple.com.

Our Daily Bread Ministries. (n.d.). *Listening to God.* Ourdailybread.com.

Parke, B. (2020, June 19). *What Does the Bible Say about Fear?* Bible Study Tools.

Piper, J. (2012, April 21). *Doing the Works of Jesus and Greater Works.*

Regoli, N. (2021, December 2). *25 Ways to Listen to God and Hear from the Lord.* Connectusfund.org.

Richert, S. (2019, January 15). *What Are the 12 Fruits of the Holy Spirit?* Learnreligions.com.

Smyth, D. (2020, February 28). *What Is the Meaning of the Lord's Prayer?* Crosswalk.com.

Today in the Word. (2020, November). Ways to be a Witness for Jesus.

Woodward, K. L. (1992, January 5). Talking to God. Newsweek.

Wellman, J. (n.d.). What Did Jesus Mean By Doing Greater Things Than These? Whatchristianswanttoknow.com.

ABOUT THE AUTHOR

Edwin (Ed) W. Thomas is the chairman and co-founder of a family office with his two sons, who have businesses including a technology and infrastructure operation focused on wastewater disposal in various industries, including oil and gas, a healthcare company focused on serving the uninsured and underinsured, and various real estate holdings.

Ed resides in Houston, Texas (Wanda, his wife of 55 years, went Home to Heaven in 2022) with his two sons (Stephen and Paul, with whom Ed is a business partner), a daughter (Suzanne, wife of the senior pastor of the 4,000 members church, Faithbridge), three Godly spouse in-laws, and eight grandchildren (born between 2004 and 2022).

Ed is a native of Hereford, Texas, graduated from Oklahoma State University with a B.S. degree in accounting/business in 1965, and played and coached NCAA football while at OSU.

For the last 50 years, Ed has been and is actively involved in several Christ-centered activities. He has been the founding President of Bible Study Ministries, founding President of the Houston Area Fellowship of Christian Athletes, on the Board of Directors of International Vision Ministries, on the elder board of Cypress Bible Church for 10 years, on the Executive Committee of Houston CoMission (Jesus Video Project), on the Advisory Board of Youth Sports International, on the Advisory Board for the Campus Crusade for Christ (CCC) Metro Ministry in Houston, co-chairman of History's Handful Latin American leadership development program, on the Executive Leadership Team for Impact XXI, on the Board of Directors of Grace School of Theology, on the Board of Impact Houston, on the Advisory Council of Lift Up America, on the Advisory Board of Crossroads, on the Latin American Ministry Council of CCC, on the Board of Directors of Enterprise Stewardship, on the Board of Cy-Hope, on the Board of ROI Ministries, on the Board of Directors of the Great Commission Foundation of CCC (CRU), on the Executive Leadership team for History's Handful, on the Advisory Board of Global Media Outreach, and founded the National Christian Foundation-Houston.

Ed has traveled (often in public speaking roles) to every US state and 93 countries, is teaching, and has taught business, home, and church Bible studies (for over 40 years).

In 2022, he was encouraged (by God through three separate people) after Wanda's going Home to Heaven to write his autobiography, "Life Journey With God," which is available on Amazon. He has written this second book, "Shoe Leather For Our Life Journey," primarily because he has personally experienced that only through God's Word can a person have an abundant and fruitful life with the Triune God.

ABOUT THE BOOK COVER

The picture on the book cover was photographed in June 2005. This is the only crevice that allows you to enter **Petra in Jordan** from the east. Petra is considered one of the seven wonders of the world. This beautiful "Rose City," which is half-carved and half-built and was once known as Raqmu, is located between the Dead Sea and the Red Sea. Petra is not only known for its famous hewn-in-the-rock monuments, but it is also one of the greatest sites in Jordan to visit for hikers and nature enthusiasts, with several walks over the cliffs and into the deep valleys inside the site.

The site is featured in multiple movies such as Indiana Jones and the Last Crusade, Arabian Nights, Passion in the Desert, Mortal Kombat: Annihilation, and Sinbad and the Eye of the Tiger.

In Tim LaHaye's and Jerry B. Jenkins' book series, "Left Behind," The Great Tribulation unfolds with one million believers under the protection of God who have fled from Satan's Antichrist and gathered in Petra which the book series identifies as the "place in the wilderness" referred to in **Revelation 12:13–17,** "*When the dragon saw that he had been thrown to earth, he persecuted the woman who gave birth to the male child. The woman was given two wings of a great eagle, so that she could fly from the serpent's presence to her **place in the wilderness**, where she was fed for a time, times, and half a time. From his mouth the serpent spewed water like a river flowing after the woman, to sweep her away in a torrent. But the earth helped the woman. The earth* *opened its mouth and swallowed up the river that the dragon had spewed from his mouth. So, the dragon was furious with the woman and left to wage war against the rest of her offspring—those who keep God's commands and have the testimony about Jesus Christ."*

Petra is an appropriate symbol of the shoe leather journey of believers under the protection, guidance, and love of a Sovereign God.

Made in the USA
Monee, IL
22 August 2023

41445827R10121